I0802053

REAL POWER

JESUS CHRIST'S AUTHORITY OVER THE SPIRITS

MOSES MATONYA

OASIS INTERNATIONAL LTD

INSIGHT BOOKS
AFRICAN ISSUES
AFRICA'S AUTHORS

Real Power

ISBN: 978-1-59452-092-1
ISBN: 1-59452-092-5

Oasis International is a ministry devoted to fostering a robust and sustainable pan-African publishing industry. For more information, go to oasisint.net.

Printed in India

Acknowledgements

I am greatly indebted to Rev. Joe Kapolyo, Principal of All Nations Christian College (UK), for his excellent idea that has resulted in the writing of this book. I was a student at All Nations for the Master of Arts degree in aspects of Christian missiology in 2001/2002 and the subject I did for the Masters dissertation was entitled, "Christology of Colossians and its implications for the Church in Tanzania today in relation to the ancestors." Wisely, Joe advised me about the need to write a book on spiritual powers and the Church in Africa after completing my course and returning to Tanzania. He suggested that I should do more research about the subject by speaking to non African Christians, ordinary Christians, pastors and Bishops to deeply understand the issue of spirits and to theologically and pastorally address it to Christians in Africa.

A very special word of thanks is offered to Langham Writers Program, for covering financial expenses of this book including researching, editing and publication costs. I am very grateful to Pieter Kwant (Langham literature) for his valuable suggestions and patient critiques and guidance that helped me to change my Masters dissertation, which is highly academic, into a book for ordinary Christian readers. Also I am thankful to Brad Palmer (Langham Writers Program) for words of encouragement and prayers from the beginning to the completion of this book. I would also like to express my special thanks to Krysia Lear (The Editorial Suite) for hard and excellent work of editing the manuscript of this book. Krysia recommended numerous changes, most of which I gratefully adopted to make the book readable to ordinary Christians.

Many special thanks to my Bishop, Rt. Rev. Mdimi Mhogolo for his challenge to theologian pastors in our Diocese of Central Tanganyika to write theological books from an African perspective for African Christian readers. His challenge has motivated me to write this book. I am also indebted to thank the tutors and students of Msalato Theological College. They shared with me the true stories and experiences related in this book. Moreover, I deeply thank my dedicated wife, Ruth, for her constant prayers and loving support that enabled this book to be written. Above all, I give thanks and praise to God, for enabling me to complete this book.

Moses Matonya
Dodoma, Tanzania

Contents

Introduction

Although the church has been established in African countries south of the Sahara for more than a century and a great many Africans continue to join the church, many African Christians practise spiritism alongside their Christian faith. People turn to the spirits to gain health, wealth and prosperity as well as to keep their jobs and businesses secure. They turn to the spirits, instead of to Jesus Christ, to protect themselves against witches, evil people and other misfortunes. They also turn to spiritism so they can maintain contact with their community and traditional culture. Those who practise spiritism include not just illiterate believers and Christians in rural areas, but also the well educated and urban dwellers, as well as some pastors and bishops.

Christians practice spiritism because they do not see Christianity as having the answers to their everyday problems. They regard Christianity as more of a social club, useful because it provides the gateway to a future life but of little relevance in the present. According to many African Christians, spirits still have the power to oppress or to bless people until Jesus Christ's second coming, after which Christians all be free from spirits' influence. In the meantime, they believe they must use their common sense in coping with the problems of everyday life, and common sense includes using the power of the spirits.

These Christians do not understand that they can turn to Jesus Christ, instead of to spirits, for the power they need because of problems in what many churches believe and teach. Some churches deny the existence of spirits and, as a result, ignore the problems Christians have with spirits. Because they expect converts to automatically abandon their traditional world view, many churches provide little relevant biblical teaching to help believers grow in their faith and deal with issues of spiritism in a Christian way. These churches dismiss those who practise spiritism as pagans, animists, superstitious, magicians and even devil worshippers. Christians in their churches who practise spiritism do so secretly fearing that their churches will condemn them. Others can be more open because their churches support the practice. One group of church leaders teaches that spirits, especially ancestral spirits, are good and influence people, including Christians, positively, so Christians can seek consult with these spirits.

Lack of practical action also contributes to problems with spiritism. African pastors rarely provide much pastoral care to ordinary Christians, so Christians do not learn about the power of Jesus. Some churches, in their opposition to indigenous beliefs and practices, have also failed to find biblical ways to keep African Christians connected to traditional values. Spiritism satisfies this need.

This practice of combining the spiritism of African traditional religion with Christianity is undermining the health of the church in Africa. If Africans are to see Christianity as a religion that meets their needs, the church must offer relevant, biblical alternatives to African Christians. To keep itself healthy, the church needs to find theological and pastoral solutions that will help people to stop practising a double-minded faith and, instead, to develop a wholehearted faith focused on Jesus Christ alone. Real Power – Jesus Christ's Authority over the Spirits shows how the African church can touch the spiritual depth of the African person. The book draws on the Bible and academic research. Material from interviews with both non-Christian and Christian Africans and church leaders in East Africa also provide lively insights and valuable examples.

Real Power first lays a foundation for what follows by providing an overview of African traditional religions to help the African church understand its power and hold on people. Then the book examines why Christians continue to practise spiritism and how the church has contributed to the problem through its theological beliefs and pastoral practices. Theologically, church leaders need to stop denying or ignoring the traditional spiritual powers because the Bible clearly accepts that supernatural powers are real, not imaginary. The Bible teaches us how to overcome these powers, both theologically and practically, through the saving power of the blood of Jesus Christ. Pastorally, it is vital for the church to offer people practical care so the spirits cannot take advantage of their fear. Such care will help to create confidence in faith in Christ, and, hence, bring maturity and total dependence on Christ alone, instead of on other powers. The church must tenderly address issues that are real to Africans in relation to their cultural and traditional religious world views, such as showing respect for family, so the message of the gospel of Jesus Christ touches the whole person.

Real Power uses the Apostle Paul's letter to the Colossians to provide biblical solutions to the problem of spiritism in the African church. Although the backgrounds of Colossae and Africa are different, the epistle is a practical resource for African Christians, both theologically and pastorally. In Colossae, as is the case in Africa, false teachings on spiritual powers threatened the faith of Christians and the health of the church. To address this problem, Paul describes the relationships between Christ and spiritual powers and speaks of Christ as the all-powerful saviour who has superiority over spiritual powers because he fully represents God in human form. Paul points out that because Christ created everything including the spirits, the spirits are under his supreme power and authority. Christ is, thus, the only saviour people need to turn to because there is provision in him for meeting both the daily spiritual and physical needs of people.

Next, the book uses the teachings in Colossians to address the faulty theology of some African churches and to show how the church can relevantly deal with the issue of the spirits. Instead of dismissing traditional values, the church can learn to understand their function. That will help the church to develop thoroughly biblical and authentically African Christian teachings and practices to uphold good values from traditional religious practices. Examples from some African churches show that it is possible to do this.

Finally, the book makes recommendations on how the church in Africa can deal biblically with the issues of spiritism among Christians.

CHAPTER ONE

Understanding the African Spirit World

While the church in Africa is vibrant and growing, the problem of many Christians turning to spirits for help with everyday life shows that it could do more to touch the spiritual depth of Africans. To do this, many church leaders and missionaries need a better understanding of the African world view regarding the influence of spirits. That will enable them to provide the teaching and pastoral support their people need to respond biblically to the spirit world. To help further this understanding, this chapter discusses the African world view on the spirit world, including the role of ancestral and non-ancestral spirits.

African World View

Spiritism continues to have such a strong hold on Christians because African religious beliefs permeate all parts of life from family to the community and political life. Religion affects daily living. In the world view of Africans, the world includes a visible realm, the part of the world that people and other creatures inhabit and a part that is invisible to human beings. Africans believe that spirits, both of ancestors and non-ancestors, inhabit the 'unseen world' and exert a great deal of influence on people's lives. They view ancestral spirits as being good and non-ancestral spirits as being evil. Even today Africans believe that these spirits can affect events in the world, in communities, and in the lives of individuals. (The differences between ancestors and are non-ancestors will be discussed in later sections.) As Samuel Ngewa says,

> *Behind ordinary things and daily events there are spirits. Sometimes this is seen as a power running through everything, but especially concentrated in anything unusual or in a special skill of a human being. This is often attributed to a host of spirits dwelling in all kinds or wandering about (1998:137).*

Followers of African traditional religions do not see spiritism as an evil and primitive practice, but rather as a search for power to meet goals in life. They seek help from spirits because they believe they cannot go directly to God. Africans commonly believe in the existence of the almighty God who is the maker of heaven and earth. They regard God as giver of life to all creatures, as all-powerful, and as the only fountain of power on Earth and above. They also regard God as remaining distant from people because he is morally good and does not like living near immoral human beings. Traditional stories of the Luo, both in Kenya and in

Tanzania, explain that God became so angry with human beings' immorality that he decided to retreat far away. Many Bantu ethnic groups like the Chagga, Zigua, Hehe, Ngoni and Nyakyusa in Tanzania believe that God shows little concern for people because human sinned against him and against other human beings and because people complained unnecessarily to him. Tired of their sins and complaints, God retired to the remote places in the heavens where he cannot be expected to interfere with the fate of people. He has, however, granted power to the spirits so they can direct and control human life on God's behalf as they like. As a result, many Africans believe they can only approach God through the mediation of intermediaries like ancestral spirits.

The Influence of the Spirits on the Lives of Africans

Economic and social conditions mean that many Africans have a real need for power. According to a World Bank report, most Africans earn less than one US dollar per day and face a daily struggle to survive. So, people at all levels of society turn to the spirits for spiritual power to get ahead. They also seek help to protect themselves from greed and destructive jealousy because people use spiritual power to harm those who are getting ahead of them, materially or socially.

To get this help, Africans frequently consult diviners and traditional medical specialists (popularly known as witchdoctors), who usually charge high rates for their services. To gain spiritual power, people place charms around the house, wear them, tie them in their clothing or have them scratched on their bodies. Sometimes, they drink magic potions or offer sacrifices to the appropriate spirits.

They seek the spirits' help for many reasons. Students in schools, colleges, and universities may rely on the spirits to protect them from witches and jealous people and to acquire extra intelligence so that they can do well in examinations. Sportsmen and sportswomen may use spirits to help them do well and to protect them from rivals. Before a big match, they may consult a diviner or local medical specialist, believing that this will help them win. Some people consult witchdoctors to avert the evil eye or to make them fertile. Senior government officials seek the spirits aid to protect them from their rivals, to enable them to perform well in their offices, and to ensure the security of their jobs. Junior officials and employees use spirits to gain favour with their superiors so that they can keep their positions and receive promotions.

Because of the influence the spirits have on people, it is very important for an African person holding this traditional world view to do or say the right thing in relation to the spirits if they want a life full of blessing and abundance. They believe that showing respect to the spirits by observing rituals, including venerating them and obeying their orders will result in blessings. They also believe that neglecting the spirits will result in misfortune and disasters such as drought, pestilence, sickness or death.

This kind of belief is very strong among the Wakamba people in Kenya, as one Kamba man told me.

They believe the spirits pervade the whole life of a person. They think that everything that happens to people must be connected to the spirits. If there is good harvest in a season, if livestock multiply and if the family is in good health, people have to praise the spirits for their good work. And if there are endless diseases and any miscarriages in the family, if there is drought or famine or if animals are naturally miscarrying because of diseases, the people will assume it is the activities of the spirits.

The Wakamba, like other who follow African traditional religions, believe that they have to consult religious specialists like diviners, traditional doctors and magicians to find the reasons for these problems and the solutions to them. Because spirits are viewed as superior to human beings, people unquestioningly obey whatever the specialists tell them to do for the spirits.

Many Africans also believe that spirits sometimes communicate directly with them by appearing as animals, particularly as one that is rare in their region. The Wakamba people of Kenya believe that the spirits appear two forms, as a person who died a long time ago and as a snake. In Tanzania, the appearance of a rare animal like a *kaka kuona* (pangolin or scaly anteater) is understood to be a spirit bringing a message. Even the media is interested in reporting such a sighting. Normally, people are expected to bring the kaka kuona items like water, food and a sword or a knife, so they can discern whether the spirit brings a good or a bad news.

If the kaka kuona drinks the water and eats the food, people will understand the message as being that the coming year will be good; there will be enough rain and people will have a good harvest. If the kaka kuona touches the sword or knife, it will then be clear to people that problems like war or epidemics are coming soon. People will then have to consult diviners and magicians to find ways to avoid the problems.

Other tribes like the Warangi, who live in Tanzania, believe that spirits can choose to appear to people as they like. They appear in the form of any domestic animal but in an unusual setting. When this happens, specialists like diviners (the *vavaiitavere* as the Warangi call them) must be consulted for the interpretation of the event.

Mr Chundu, a member of the Warangi, said that a friend, who was alone in a forest earlier this year, suddenly saw a goat grazing freely on its own. The sight frightened him because it is unusual to see a domestic animal in that remote place because animals like lions and hyenas inhabited the area. He reported this incident to his parents and they went to see the vavaiitavere to understand the meaning of the event. The diviner told them that what the boy had seen was not an ordinary goat but was a spirit of an ancestor who wanted a goat sacrificed in his memory.

Ancestral Spirits and their Significance

What are the ancestral spirits?

Africans believe that in the passage to death, God the Almighty grants special power to the living dead (especially ancestral spirits) for the sake of their families on earth.

With this power, ancestral spirits can mediate between God and people; they can channel God's blessings to people and can protect them from dangers. Because kinship is every important, many ethnic groups and tribes in East Africa regard ancestral spirits as family members in a spirit form who continue to influence the lives of people known to them. Ancestors are concerned with the welfare of their communities, so they remain involved with their people. Because communion with ancestors is so important, many non-Africans have assumed that Africans worship their dead ancestors. Rather Africans communicate with them as though they were still living. For their part, ancestors continue to communicate with their families through dreams and appearances as animals.

Although Africans believe that after their physical death, all people take on a spirit form and remain closely connected with them spiritually, they do not regard every one who dies as an 'ancestor.' To be an ancestor, a person must fulfil certain conditions. The person must have led a morally good life in accordance with traditional standards of the society concerned. He or she should have been peacemakers in the community and exemplars of fostering communion between the living and the living dead through prayers and sacrifices. The person also needs to have descendants.

Descendents are important because they perform the ritual services that confer ancestorhood on people and that maintain ancestors in that state. Children ensure that the ancestors are remembered, which allows ancestors to continue participating in human life. For an African, not having children, particularly sons, is the worst curse. Sons not only ensure that their parents (ancestors) are remembered, as do daughters, but because of the patriarchal system, they also ensure the continuation of the clan through their children. The curse for the childless person is pronounced at the burial ceremony when elders condemn the barrenness. The Wagogo people say, '*Bite no wubi wako nha si ulaleceza wanji mu mbeyu yenyu*,' which means 'Go with your shame and no one in your extended family should be like you.'

For people to remain ancestors, their descendants must regularly communicate with them through prayer and sacrificial offerings. Some African tribes believe that a firstborn son is a candidate par excellence to become an ancestor because he is able to maintain the chain of generations in a long genealogy. A firstborn daughter also can become an ancestress if she meets the qualifications, but because of the patriarchal system, she cannot maintain the chain of generations.

Many ethnic groups, however, like the Wasukuma of Tanzania, believe that any person, whether male or female and not necessarily the firstborn, is qualified to become an ancestor on the condition that they have children of their own. The Wagogo people of Tanzania believe that both women and men who have children serve as ancestors not only to their descendants but also to others with whom they have a blood relationship, such as nieces and nephews.

Other tribes like the Wanyamwanga and Wasafwa in southwestern Tanzania consider dead chiefs, kings and warriors of the tribes to be tribal ancestors. When certain problems affect the whole tribe, people cry out to their tribal ancestors for help. The first president of Tanzania, Julius Nyerere is treated as having ancestral responsibilities for his people.

What is the significance of the ancestral spirits?

With the power that the ancestors have and with the spiritual qualities that allow them to be anywhere, Africans believe that nothing can escape their attention. They are concerned with the welfare of their people. The Wasukuma people in Tanzania believe that all human success and misfortune is subject to the ancestor's influence (Ngewa 1998:135). The ancestors generally bless their earthly families, but can cause problems for them.

Because the ancestors generally influence life positively, properly communing with the spirits of the ancestors results in fullness of life or the well-being of a person on earth and in the world to come. The fullness of life refers to a situation in which a person is blessed with children, is healthy, and is not handicapped in any way. He or she has complete peace and anticipates fully participating in another honourable life in the world of the spirits. Thus, when everything is as it should be in a person's life, it indicates that this person enjoys a good relationship with the spirits of his or her ancestors.

Ancestors can provide fullness of life for three reasons, because they serve as mediators between God and their earthly kin, because they are responsible for their families, and because they influence the social well-being of people. Africans believe they need the ancestors to speak to God on their behalf.

As mediators, ancestors communicate with God on their family's behalf. To differentiate between God and other spirits, the Wagogo people call the spirits, particularly ancestral spirits, *milungu* and believe their function is to mediate in any communications between the almighty God (*Mulungu U Mulungulungu*) and the people on earth. According to Gehman, in Kenya, various Wakamba speak of the ancestors as being nearer to God and, therefore, possessing better knowledge of God and having better access to him than the living. The living can only approach God through the ancestors (Gehman 2002:154).

The Wanguu people in Tanzania regard the ancestors as living spirits that are endowed with special powers and abilities by the Supreme God for the sake of the people related to them. As spirits, ancestors know the languages of both God and humans. The Wanguu, therefore, believe in the ancestors as reconcilers between God and the people and as intermediaries who bring peoples' problems to God and bring back the answers from God to the people.

In describing how the Wasafwa understand the relationship between people, ancestors and God, Mr Mwanjela, says that the spirits of the ancestors are the bridges of communication between God and people on earth. Similarly, the Waburunge people in Central Tanzania understand the ancestors (*Ilitlemamee*) as spirits whose duty is to make the link between God and people possible. They receive orders from God and take them to the people. A person is, therefore, obliged to have good relationships with the ancestors so that they do not cut off this link between God and themselves.

With this understanding, many Africans equate the role of ancestors with that of holy angels in the Bible. According to Hebrews 1:14, angels are spirits; they are also known as the heavenly host (Ps. 103:20–21; 148:2–5). Like ancestral spirits, angels live in the invisible world (in heaven) and act as God's messengers to human beings. Because they have this role, God also grants angels power and authority.

However, ancestral spirits seem to be more important to Africans than angels are in the Bible. Ancestral spirits are mediators between God and the people, while angels are just God's messengers. Also, ancestors are closely related to people because they were human beings. They are, thus, more responsible to people than are angels, who are created as spirits and whose have a distant relationship with human beings. More importantly, ancestors are free to use the special power and authority they are granted by God as they like, whereas angels are not given that kind of freedom. They cannot use their power and authority outside God's will. Many Africans still believe what R.F. Schreiter wrote more than ten years ago:

> *It was to the ancestors that God first communicated the divine 'vital force.' Thus they constitute the highest link, after God, in the chain of beings. But they still remain human beings. In their death passage, they have become*

> *more powerful than other human beings in their capacity to exert influence, to increase or to diminish the vital force of earthly beings. In their present state, they behold both God and God's subjects (117–118).*

Second, ancestors can provide fullness of life because they are responsible to protect their families and make sure there is harmony between members of their families. Many Africans still regard the spirits, particularly the ancestral spirits, as the ones who control life and are authentic guardians of moral order and customs in the society. The presence of ancestors is the basis for unity and authority in each family and society. Ancestors are not pleased when there is conflict and disagreement between people in the family and when such problems persist, the ancestors intervene to bring harmony. The Waburunge believe they bring plagues on the people involved in a disagreement. So, if a plague occurs, they will ask a diviner to interpret its meaning and to stop the punishment. They have to reconcile and to kill an animal as a sacrifice and ask the ancestors for forgiveness.

Third, ancestors can provide fullness of life because they have power and influence over the social well-being of people. Many Africans believe that God has granted the ancestors powers to which people can appeal for help in meeting their daily needs. Africans believe that because of the special powers ancestors can channel God's various blessings such as rain, long life, wealth, many wives and many children to them. People believe that ancestors are the source of victory in war, in legal cases, in political elections and even in singing competitions and sports.

The belief that ancestors have power to protect people and their livestock from sickness and other calamities exists in my extended family. In 1979, my brother lost all our cattle on the mountain where he was grazing them. We searched for them for two nights and two days, with no success. Our grandfather, who was not a Christian at that time, had gone to a diviner to learn the cause of this problem and whether the cattle were still safe or had been stolen or killed by wild animals. The diviner told him that his family had no problems with the ancestors, and the ancestors were protecting the animals on the mountain. The diviner assured him that we would find all the cattle safe the next day. When we returned we found him calm and he told us everything the diviner had been said including the paths to use early the following morning. We did as he told us and found the animals safe.

Because of their influence and because they are the guardians of moral order and customs in the society, ancestors are regarded as the source of life. Because of that and because of the special power God has given them, people are supposed to venerate the ancestors. The Wahangaza people believe they must be at peace with the ancestors at all times to gain the ancestors' favour. The best way of making peace is to maintain communion with the ancestors, often through libations, festivals, ritual offerings and prayer. There is no unified system among tribes and families for carrying out these activities. The important thing is to follow the instructions the family gets from a practitioner like a diviner or witch doctor.

As described earlier, ancestors are normally friendly to their earthly families. When respected, they provide blessings and abundance, but sometimes, especially when their descendants fail to render them appropriate honour, they bring trouble. They are said to manifest their spiritual anger by sending calamities like death and diseases to their descendants' families and livestock. Many Africans believe they are to offer a sacrifice to the ancestors when something is wrong. When something like a drought affects the community, the whole community needs to raise its voice to the ancestors. Rainia, a diviner from the Zanaki tribe in Tanzania, described such an event, which occurred about thirteen years ago. Quoted by Kirwen (1987:33), Riana says:

> *Last year, for example, when rain failed, the elders of the people gathered at the Mirari River where they sacrificed a goat to the ancestors and prayed that the ancestors would look kindly upon them and give them rain. There was no doubt in their minds that this evil had happened because the ancestors were holding their protecting power and punishing the living for their immorality. They prayed: 'Young grandfathers, don't be angry. Our evils are many in the land where you have brought us. Forgive us. Take them away from us-bring peace and blessing. Give us rain. May all the children grow up, the cattle be fertile, the boys and girls be well—bless us all.' All left convinced that they had attained their purpose of appeasing the ancestors. And the rain did come.*

In 2001, a local doctor called Busla, who lives in Ilii-Mooraa village in Waburunge land, gave the people in the village a message from the ancestors, saying that they were angry because people had forgotten them. To appease this anger, Busla explained that they needed to sacrifice a black lamb to the ancestors. Disobedience would cause a disaster that would kill many people, pregnant women in particular. The people did not obey and the result was the death of sixteen pregnant women in the village.

Last year, a woman told to me that she suddenly had serious eye disease. She went to several hospitals, including Mvumi Hospital in Dodoma, which specialises in treating eye diseases, but with no success. She was then taken to the church for healing prayers. This did not help. Later, her family consulted the local witchdoctor and discovered that the ancestors were punishing her because she and her family had forsaken them by becoming Christians. The family made a sacrifice to the ancestors to ask their forgiveness and, finally, the woman's eyes recovered. Because of this, both she and her family still continue to venerate the ancestors though they are Christians.

Among the Wakamba in Kenya, as Mukamba told me, a living person is supposed to follow the customs of the family according to the instructions of elders. Failure to do so may result in the ancestors reacting angrily. Every crisis that develops after that, whether it is sickness or death, drought or pestilence, will be regarded as being caused by the ancestors.

According to the Wagogo, ancestral spirits can reveal the things that are about to happen so people can prepare for good things or take precautions in case of bad things. An infertile Indian woman in Dodoma, who wanted to have children, went with her husband to several big hospitals in Tanzania and Kenya, but without any success. A man at Kitelela Village, about 25 kilometres from Dodoma, who did not know her was instructed by *mizimu ya mababu* (spirits of the ancestors) to go to a big tree in a river to get its roots for a medication to enable the woman to have children. Although this man did not know the woman and her problem, the spirit directed him to the woman. He told her everything that the spirits had told. She used the medicine she was given, finally she had a son who is alive even today (as it is told).

Non-Ancestral Spirits and their Functions

Non-ancestral spirits are always evil, harmful and associated with witches, sorcerers, magicians and superstitious people of dealing with evil spirits. Beliefs about non-ancestral spirit vary widely. Some tribes believe both kinds of spirits exist, while other tribes believe only ancestral spirits exist and that all spirits including the unknown ones have their origin in the ancestors. Some tribes believe that non-ancestral spirits are the spirits of the forgotten ones, forgotten in the sense that they are long-departed people, who are not remembered by any living person.

A similar view is that non-ancestral spirits consist of two types of spiritual elements. The first group consists of human spirits or ghosts (in Swahili *mizimu ya wahenga*).

These are the dead who have passed out of the memory of the living. They could be the spirits of children, brothers, and sisters who passed away without proper initiation. They could also be the spirits of men and women, who either died without children or who did not receive a proper burial, either because others believed they were as witches or because they had died away from home. The Luo people in both Kenya and Tanzania call these kinds of human spirits *abasambwa*. The second group of non-ancestral spirits is non-human. In Swahili, they are known as *mapepo* or *pepo*. They are the spirits of dead animals and of some spirits that were created as such.

Like ancestral spirits, non-ancestral spirits can operate freely so they are able to empower anybody, as they like. They are the ones who direct and use people as they desire. According to traditional belief, when spirits empowers people they can lead people wherever they want them to go. They could lead a person even at night to go to a mountain to find medicine and keep the person there for any period of time, even for a month, without the person eating and drinking.

What are the functions of non-ancestral spirits?

Generally, Africans fear non-ancestral spirits because they believe they are very destructive and they fear them more than they do ancestral spirits because they believe that non-ancestral spirits are more harmful than ancestral spirits. Some people would not even discuss the subject with me for fear that non-ancestral spirits would react angrily causing great trouble for them and their families. People believe the non-ancestral spirits are so destructive because they lived that way on earth and continue to act as they did before they died. In addition, people believe that, the non-ancestral spirits are likely to take revenge and cause evil things to happen because they were not treated well at their burial. Non-ancestral spirits normally destroy life by bringing calamities on people like drought, starvation, serious disease and death.

The belief that non-ancestral spirits departed a long time ago and that people have forgotten them is the reason that people like the Wasukuma find them terribly fearsome. In ordinary circumstances, these spirits receive no recognition through prayers or sacrifices because they are not ancestors (Magesa 1997:56). Therefore, the best way they can attract attention from people is to cause trouble.

Mapepo, the non-human spirits, are feared as being even more dangerous than non-ancestral human spirits because they are believed to be associated with magic and witchcraft. Evil people, like sorcerers and bad magicians, use them to harm someone they envy or hate. Others who want to use these spirits to harm and even kill others have to pay something, for example money or a cow, to the sorcerer or magician.

Normally, non-human spirits cause humans to have health problem. According to many tribes, a person possessed by mapepo would be noticed because they exhibit uncontrollable behaviour and would be in serious pain. In addition, they would do unpredictable things such as dancing akin to having the shakes or would carry out a rash act like butchering an animal without the ordinary process of decision and preparation. They do such things involuntarily because they are unable to carry on their normal duties.

According to the Akamba people, writes Gehman (2002:158):

> *Spirit possession usually begins by someone starting to cry for no reason. Or he may have an abnormal sickness, like a headache, which is accompanied by loud crying or running away from home. There is general agreement that during the transition period, as the person passes into the state of possession, there is a feeling of going numb throughout the whole body. The person becomes weak as his bodily strength declines. Darkness grips the mind. When one is fully possessed, he demonstrates the power of aimu (spirits). He demonstrates unusual physical strength … the possessed may walk on fire without being burned, cut himself without being hurt or eat dangerous fruits without being sick.*
>
> *Some of these non-ancestral spirits, if treated well, will help those who seek their help.*

According to many Africans, non-ancestral spirits can help a person find treasure and other things of benefit through witchcraft, a practice carried out very secretly. A rich man claims that his success is due to the work of non-ancestral spirits. When he asked a sorcerer to help him become rich, the sorcerer agreed on the condition that he supply about 10 litres of human blood to feed the spirits the sorcerer kept. The sorcerer said that when they were fed well with the human blood, the spirits would lead the man treasure. To meet the condition, the rich man killed a person; the spirits led him to a mountain where he found diamonds in a basket. He sold the diamonds and bought buses and lorries, a business he still has.

On 19 September 2003, *Nipashe*, a daily newspaper in Tanzania, carried a story on another attempt to use witchcraft to get rich. The newspaper reported that the police caught two naked men in Arusha Town with the body of a dead woman aged 25 in their car. They were taking the body either to the sea or to a lake. These two men had been instructed by a local witchdoctor (in Swahili *mange way kienyeji*) that, if they wanted to be rich, they should kill one of their girlfriends and throw her body into the sea to feed the spirits who live there, and that they should complete this exercise while naked. When the police arrested the mganga wa kienyeji, they found him working at home as a local doctor and people queuing to see him for help.

The belief in *jinn*, a type of non-human spirit, is also popular in Africa, especially along the East African coast. The belief in jinni was brought to East Africa by Arab traders beginning in the eighth century. As the trade flourished, Arabs established settlements and infused their civilisation into that of the East Africans. According to Arab tales, jinni, who were created from fire as spirits, can appear in visible and invisible forms and, if visible, both in the shape of an animal or a human, especially as a beautiful woman who can attract men to have sexual relations with her. Most jinni are considered bad spirits.

Many people I interviewed said that they live among human beings and that when they appear it usually dangerous for humans because they cause harm and, sometimes, death.

Some jinni, provided they are treated well, will do good for humans and help them to succeed. Some people have become rich because of their relationship with good jinni. However, some who disobeyed these jinni have been severely punished. The number of good jinni, however, are few compared to the number of evil ones.

Non-ancestral spirits can also inhabit humans and harm them. Spirits do not inhabit every person in a family and or a society. However, spirits, especially ancestral spirits, can enter certain people whenever they want by intrusion to either help and for harm. Non-ancestral spirits also enter people for bad and good reasons but some, especially the jinn, enter people on command of sorcerers and magicians, who are fulfilling customers' requests to harm enemies and opponents.

When they invade a person, good spirits always cause good things to the person. They might enable the person to prosper in business or other activities, to pass with high outstand in all examinations, to become employed and to marry and have healthy children. Bad spirits always cause problems, such as misfortune, illness, confusion, and even death, for the people they inhabit. To stop these spirits from causing harm, people try to either expel them or appease them. To get rid of spirits, some people, in consultation with diviners and good magicians, appeal to ancestral spirits for help through prayers and ritual offerings. Many

Africans believe that ancestors' powers are superior to those of non-ancestral spirits and strong enough to ward off the evil spirits. Other people acquire preventive magical powers like charms from diviners and magicians to neutralise, take revenge on or to expel the evil spirits. Those who try to appease the spirits might use prayer and sacrifice as signs that they have surrendered to the power of the spirits and are asking for mercy. The spirits would be pleased by such honour and would be willing to depart from the victims. Other people satisfy the claims of the spirits that have attacked them. Still others make friends with these spirits. Following the instructions of the diviner, 'a permanent relationship is ritually established between spirits and victim that involves possession of the victims by the spirits' (Lane 1996:119). Normally, people build friendships with the spirits by providing them with food they like and by placating them with offerings and sacrifices. Some spirits require blood from a member of the victim's family, which means killing a relative, as happens among the Wagogo.

In summary, it can be said that in general Africans still believe that spirits of both the ancestors and non-ancestors affect all events, whether for good or bad, in the life of individuals and communities. As Ngewa observed among the tribes around Lake Victoria in Tanzania,

> *Behind ordinary things and daily events, there are spirits. Sometimes this is seen as power running through everything, but especially concentrated in anything unusual or in a special skill of a human being. This power is often attributed to a host of spirits dwelling in all kinds of place, or wandering about (1998:137).*

Because of the influence spirits have, many Africans, including Christians, believe that if they want a life filled with blessing, it is important to have good relationships not only with God but also with the spirits. They believe that showing respect for the spirits by carrying out various rituals results in abundance of life, while neglecting the spirits brings misfortune and calamity.

CHAPTER TWO

Spirits and the Church in Africa

Two factors have largely influenced African Christians to retain traditional religious practices. One is the widespread influence of traditional African religions in society and its impact on African Christians. The other is the way the church in Africa has dealt, theologically and pastorally, with the role of the Christ and the role of spirits in the church.

The Influence of the Spirits on African Christians

As the Introduction points out, many African Christians, both urban and rural, end up leading double lives because their world view and roots go deep in traditional religious practices. They adhere both to Christianity and to traditional religions, mainly the cults of spirits, because they continue to believe that spirits have real power to affects everybody, including themselves, and all areas of life. Although they regularly attend church, they still lead their lives in ways that satisfy their spiritual and physical needs. A Christian man whose son is an evangelist in the church in Chambalo Village in Kondoa, Tanzania is a good example of this. This farmer, who is one of the wealthiest people in the area, says he is rich because of his good relationships with his ancestors. Every year near the rainy season, he sacrifices a black lamb to his ancestors to ask for blessings and good harvest. Because he succeeds every year, he continues with the practice and is not shy about it. Some church leaders and educated Christians carry out similar practices; indeed some have been discovered running their ministries and organizations under the protection of the spirits.

Christians turn back to the spirits in many ways. They use the names of their ancestors for religious purposes. They hang idols of spirits in their homes, in their workplaces, including offices, farms, market places and shops, and in their vehicles. Christians wear charms and amulets to prevent themselves from being harmed by superstitious people. I remember the day I had to remove charms (*hirizi* in Swahili) from seven of twenty children I was to baptise in church one Sunday. Some of the parents who brought the children would have been wearing them as well.

Sometimes the truth is revealed in dramatic ways. One pastor told me about a man who gave his testimony following the sermon, saying that Christ was his Lord and shield. As he stood talking, a sudden powerful wind blew from outside through the church, lifted his robe and uncovered the upper part of his body. People saw a charm on his shoulder, which revealed, to his a great embarrassment, that his testimony was untrue.

Christian laypeople are not the only ones who turn to spirits. Some Christian choirs use spiritual powers and magic to enable them to sing better than other choirs. Some pastors and bishops seek the spirits' aid so they can do well. Moreover, some pastors fear the activities of the spirits and of evil spirits, in particular. They fear, for example, that if they exorcise Christians who are disturbed by the spirits, they will offend the spirits and jeopardise themselves. Some pastors have magic scratches to enable them to see evil spirits and wizards at night so that they can chase them away.

Because of the traditional view of the omnipresence of the spirits, some churches believe that evil spirits could be present inside their church buildings. They have to cast them out in prayer in the name of Jesus to purify the church before they start their services. The prediction that the belief in the spirits will continue to exist in this millennium if the church does not address it clearly is true (Molyneux 2001:5).

Why are the Spirits a Problem among African Christians?

Because the church does not address the theological and pastoral issues related to the power of spirits or speak to their deepest needs and fears, many African believers feel it is safer to keep both their Christian faith and traditional beliefs rather than to abandon traditional beliefs completely. This problem with spirits exists among African Christians for three reasons: misunderstanding about Jesus' power and role, the belief that ancestors are responsible for the welfare of the kin group and a lack of sound teaching from the Bible about the spirit world.

First, many African Christians assume that the power of the spirits can work alongside the power of Jesus in their lives, especially in times of desperate need. They will ask a pastor or fellow Christian to pray for them in the name of Jesus Christ and will also consult the power of the spirits, hoping to get immediate help to supplement the prayers they have received in the name of Jesus. They do this because they do not understand that Jesus Christ is all-powerful, that he has power over the spirits and that he, alone, is able to take care of their greatest needs or difficulties. Their faith has remained immature despite the fact that Christianity has existed in Africa south of the Sahara for more than a century.

Second, for anthropological reasons, the fear of spirits is real. Africans are very conscious of their ties to the community and of belonging to an extended family, a family that consists of the living and the dead. The latter means Africans believe they must maintain good relationships with their ancestors because they play a significant role in their own fortunes and misfortunes. They also want to maintain good relationships because their ancestors' presence is the basis for the unity and authority of the family. It, therefore, becomes very difficult for African Christians to cut themselves off from the spirits because, by denying the ancestors, they automatically isolate themselves from their family ties. They fear that the ancestral spirits may react very angrily.

In addition, they fear that losing contact with their ancestors will leave them unprotected from the destructive powers of evil spirits and those who use those powers. So, when a crisis like death, sickness or another misfortunes occurs, their interpretation of the cause is based on this world view and they swiftly resort to the practices and beliefs of traditional religions.

Evelina from Dabalo, a village in the Dodoma region of Tanzania, provides a good example of a Christian who loved the Lord Jesus Christ for many years and yet turned back to the spirits. When her father, a local witchdoctor, was about to die he told her that the spirits of their ancestors were going to empower her to become a witchdoctor after his death. Evelina refused to accept this because it was against her Christian faith. Her father did not change his message because he perceived it as an order from their ancestors. As soon as her father died, the spirits started to visit Evelina in dreams and visions, even during the daylight hours. They insisted that she should obey them and started leading her by force to the nearby mountain at night. She also became seriously ill with unknown diseases. She finally obeyed the commands of the spirits and she became a mganga wa kienyeji. She continues with this work and her faith has weakened. The church knows about it but has not done anything to help her. Christians like Evelina are quite common in East Africa.

Loyi, an elderly woman, is another example of a Christian who practices spiritism alongside her Christian faith. She calls herself a committed Christian who attends church regularly and comes from a Christian family. Her brother is a pastor in the Anglican church in Dodoma in Tanzania. This woman is also a local medical specialist in women's diseases related to fertility Loyi told me that her profession has been successful because the spirits of her two aunts gave her the skill to be a herbalist to help infertile women. The spirits continue appearing and speaking to her in visions and dreams about the problems of women who were coming and the medicine that would cure their problems.

In explaining how the spirits started to communicate with her, Loyi said that one day in 1967, around midday, she saw two women dressed in white who told her that she must become a herbalist to help infertile women have children. She did not pay attention, but the spirits appeared to her again and again with the same message and gave her their names. She told her parents and mentioned the names of the spirits, which her parents recognised as the names of her aunts who had been local herbalists. Loyi obeyed their voices. Since then Loyi has become very famous and people come to her from all over Tanzania and as far as India and Arabia for help. She showed me a list of people she has helped; it included a student at Msalato Bible College, whose wife now has a baby boy. Loyi is licensed by the government and often she visits the hospitals in Dodoma Town to lead seminars for nurses and midwives on women's diseases that cause infertility. Sometimes doctors from the hospitals seek her advice when they are not sure whether they should operate.

Between 1993 and 1995 when I was the parish vicar of Kigwe Village in the Dodoma region, people told me that a man who was a Christian and church elder was also a witchdoctor. I asked him about this and he confirmed that he was. When I advised him that it is not good for a Christian to be a witchdoctor, he accepted the advice but refused to stop for fear that the mizimu that made him a witchdoctor would kill him. It was difficult for him to refuse their orders and he is still a witchdoctor.

Third, many Christians in Africa lack contextual biblical teaching about the Christian faith, especially in relation to their spiritual world. As a result, the message of the gospel does not speak to their deepest needs and fears. African Christians expect that God will work more powerfully, genuinely and quickly in their daily lives than the spirits will. Therefore, it becomes unrealistic for them to wait patiently for answers to their prayers as the church teaches them to do. When they do not get swift answers, turning to the spirits become the obvious alternative. Many African Christians from traditional religious backgrounds believe that the spirits are quicker to answer the needs of people than God is.

A pastor said this happened during a drought in Umbulu in Tanzania that continued although Christians had been praying for rain in their churches for several weeks. People went to a rainmaker, who told them that the ancestors had caused the drought. He advised them to sacrifice a black lamb to the ancestor and then find a beautiful girl for him to marry and it would soon rain. They did this and, in three days, the rain came. According to the pastor, this incident caused many Christians to trust more in the spirits and the rainmaker than in Christ. Early in

2003 during a widespread drought in Tanzania, we saw Christians and non-Christians asking rainmakers for rain. Some Christians are also rainmakers.

The belief that the spirits are more powerful than Christ is also based on the traditional view that God cannot easily get involved in people's affairs because he is so far away. Christians I interviewed said that God was quicker to answer them through ancestral mediation than he through Christianity. When they had heard that Jesus Christ is the true representation of God himself, they had responded unquestioningly to the call to believe in him. They had expected that, because Christ Jesus is the Son of God, he would be more powerful than other spiritual powers and that he would bring the fullness of life to believers and their families. To them, this meant that Jesus Christ would be the source of blessings and would completely defeat the evil and sufferings that harassed them. However, they found that Christ's power was not demonstrated in their daily affairs, especially in times of difficulty and suffering. Christians in Africa are, thus, easily convinced that even in Christianity, God's power is still inaccessible to human. So Christianity has not changed many Africans.

How the Church has Dealt Theologically with the Role of Christ and the Role of the Spirits in the Church in Africa

Spirits are also a problem because African churches do not provide strong biblical teaching about them; some churches deny the existence of spirits. A Moravian pastor told me that the church does not like to teach about spirits because there is nothing good to be found in them. He said that the 'so-called spirits' are just psychological problems people have and that spirits do not actually exist. The pastor insisted that when these problems become serious a person becomes disturbed mentally and acts as if he or she is possessed by spirits.

Those who believe in the existence of spirits hold a variety of beliefs. One group says that no human spirits exist, but that God created good spirits to watch over people in families and communities and to mediate between himself and the people on earth in the age of darkness before the coming of Jesus Christ. The coming of Christ marked the end of the role of these spirits. Most of the Christians who believe that spirits operated as forerunners to Christ think that angels and other spiritual powers mentioned in the Bible and the ancestral spirits in African traditional religions belong to this group. Concerning evil spirits, they say the non-ancestral spirits like mapepo and jinn and other destructive spirits are just bad spirits and are the forces of Satan that are working against the will of God. The belief is that these spirits can possess superstitious people and magicians and are always enemies of human beings. The good news, according to those who hold this view, is that these spirits are inferior to the good spirits of God and are even more inferior to and powerless against committed Christians. Speaking emphatically, Godian Katwaza, an evangelist in Kagera, Tanzania, said that Christians do not have to worry about evil spirits because they are surrounded by the supreme power of Jesus, which protects them from the destructive forces of the evil one.

A similar view holds that spirits were created, but are not ancestral spirits or other human spirits. Rev. Ulumye of the Moravian Church in Tabora in Tanzania, who described this view, said that because people and Christians have little knowledge about spirits they have assumed their dead relatives are some of these spirits. Ulumye says that God created spirits to guide and discipline people until Christ came to bring the light from God. This is the light that saves believers completely from sin and all difficulties in life on earth caused by Satan and his evil forces. Ulumye said that, before Christ came, spirits had power to punish and reward people according to their deeds; after he came, Christ, who does these things to a greater extent, took over the spirits' responsibilities. Spirits are, thus, powerless and functionless for committed Christians. According to Ulumye, the role of the church is to teach this to Christians and to all people so that they put a strong focus on Jesus Christ and stop thinking about spirits. This will help Christians not to be affected by spirit-related problems.

A second view is that ancestral spirits are not spirits as such, but are, somehow, God's ways of involving himself in human life. Supporters of the view would say that God partially manifested himself to the people as an ancestral spirit in the form of a creature to help people in an ordinary human way. Now that Christ has come, God does not need to manifest himself as spirit. Christ, as God-man, reveals God fully and he deals with all spiritual and physical needs of a person more fully than the spirits. Christians who criticize this view, say it is biblically incorrect because it lowers God so much to the level of human spirits. In the Bible, God is described as the creator of angels who are his messengers to the people on earth and to watch over them (Ps 34:7; Dan 6:22; Heb 1:14). Even in many African traditional religions, God has a unique position as creator of spirits and is the only One who grants them limited to mediate between him and people and to involve themselves in the daily social needs of people on his behalf.

The third view holds that spirits exist and ancestral spirits are good and influence people, including Christians, positively. As a result, those who accept the view believe it is not sinful for Christians to practice ancestral spiritism because the result is love, unity, peace and good life for them and others in the community. However, this view does not support the practice of venerating non-ancestral spirits because, normally, they are evil and destructive. A leading official in the Moravian church of Tanzania favours this view, saying that it is not sin for a Christian to communicate with ancestral spirits and to respect their advice. His point is that ancestors are our parents and their parental responsibilities do not stop when they die, but continues in an even better way because they have become spiritual beings and can now intercede with God. This belief is quite popular among Roman Catholic African Christians; the Roman Catholic Church regards its saints as spirits through whom prayers of Christians can be channelled to Christ the supreme mediator and finally to God.

The belief has even spread to Christians of evangelical Protestant churches. Rev. Isaiah Chambala, an Anglican priest and teacher of theology at Munguishi Christian Training Centre, supports the view. Chambala uses the Bible to justify the view. He says that ancestors revealed the use of herbal medicines that heal our diseases and that communicating with the spirits is biblical. His first reference is from 1 Samuel 28:14–20 which tells of the time that King Saul, who was in trouble because of the Philistine army, sought advice from the dead Samuel. Samuel appeared to him as spirit wearing a robe and told him that the Philistines would surely defeat him because God was allowing them to punish Saul because of his sin. Therefore, says Chambala, although he was dead, Samuel continued to play his role as judge. His second example is from the gospel of Luke 9:28–34. Moses and Elijah, who had lived centuries earlier, appeared to the transfigured Jesus to talking about his death at Jerusalem, which would fulfil God's plan for the salvation of the world. In 2002, Chambala did simple research on attitudes to ancestors in his former parish church at Kiteto. In a confidential survey, Christians were to write yes or no on a sheet of paper in answer to his question: 'Would you like the practice of ancestors to be allowed in the church?' According to him, 95 per cent said yes and 5 per cent said no, which clearly indicates that many Christians do not find that it is wrong to honour spirits.

Also, many Christians in Tanzania have said that it right for people like Julius Nyerere, the first president of Tanzania, to continue his ancestral responsibilities for his people. When Tanzanians were commemorating the fourth year of Nyerere's death in 2003, some Protestant bishops and ordinary Christians, together with Roman Catholic colleagues, appeared on television, asking Nyerere, in prayer, to continue his role as a mediator with God. They wanted him to do this that the peace, love and unity he had established would continue and the country might prosper economically.

At the Anglican Cathedral of the Holy Spirit in Dodoma in October 2003, I witnessed the pastor in charge of the service pray for three respected old Christian ladies who had brought an offering for a spirit to the service. While sitting quietly at home, one of the ladies had suddenly seen a white woman standing in front of her and recognised her as a teacher at Mvumi Girls School in early 1940s who had died. The white woman said to her that the ladies had forgotten her and must give an offering in the church in remembrance of her. These ladies gave their offering in the church, and the pastor thanked God for the life of their teacher and for her appearance to these ladies, who regarded it as a momentous occasion.

This view honours to the spirits and does not place Christ at a unique position as the only mediator between God and people. As a result, it is contrary to the will of God and is not helpful in enabling Christians grow in their knowledge about God and in their dependence in Christ Jesus.

Benezet Bujo, a Catholic theologian in Congo-Kinshasa and an African writer, says that Christ Jesus has displaced the role of spirits for African Christians. By his death and resurrection, Christ has become the means of God's salvation. He has defeated sin and death that enslaved humanity for a long time and has brought into being a new creation. Spirits are just forerunners of Christ, but Christ is now the real saviour (Bujo 1992:80–83). Similar to Bujo's view is that of many students of Msalato Bible College in Dodoma in Tanzania. They say that by his incarnation, death and resurrection, Jesus has assumed supreme authority and power to redeem people from the evil powers and social oppression. Christians, therefore, should no longer fear evil spirits because Jesus Christ protects them. Through individual and community prayer and worship, they say that sacred contact can be maintained between Christ and Christians for unity and for social and spiritual issues.

Another view argues that Jesus Christ has replaced the mediatory function of our natural spirit fathers and become the final and completing element that crowns the traditional religiosity of Africans. An African writer and Protestant theologian in Ghana Kwame Bediako supports this view saying that by his death, resurrection and ascension Jesus has assumed a singular importance. He has returned to the realm of the ancestral spirits as Lord over all spirits and powers in much the same way that he is Lord over the living on earth. He is, therefore, the Lord and judge over the living and the dead and over the spirits.

Many Christians support this last view, arguing that the practice of spiritism is both sinful and useless. (Sadly, they do not all practice what they believe.) The practice is sinful because it is idolatrous. It useless because, although God helped them only with great tolerance when they practised spiritism before becoming Christians, now God can help them through Jesus Christ. Believing in Christ and studying the Bible has let them clearly see God's light, which shows them how evil the practice of spiritism is for Christians. Rev. Canon Richard Chomolla of the Anglican Church says that the practice of spiritism is for non-Christians who have not discovered the light of God in Christ. Christians, he says, should not continue to depend on the spirits because the Lord Jesus Christ is able to help them more than the spirits can and the spirits become completely powerless to affect Christians. Further explaining the view, an evangelist Samson Bisakumbwa of Kigoma in Tanzania says that it is sinful for a Christian to continue believing in the spirits because, to a great extent, the belief in the spirits involves the power of Satan. According to Rev. Alexander Ulumye of the Moravian church in Tabora, Tanzania, the belief is sinful because it involves consultation with diviners and magicians and this is idolatry.

How the Church has Dealt with Pastorally with the Role of Christ and the Role of the Spirits in the Church in Africa

Pastorally, the church in Africa has also dealt poorly with the issue of spiritism. It has not provided biblical teaching that enable Christians to mature in their faith or that relates to their lives. Nor has the church provided the care that relates to daily needs or helps Christians preserve the good values from their traditional beliefs. For different reasons, mainline Protestant and Pentecostal churches have a negative attitude towards traditional religious practices, including adherence to the spirits. This attitude has affected their missions' programmes, which the churches use to try to destroy all traditional religious values. They want to make sure that all African Christians completely abandoned the practice of spiritism. Pastor Joseph Kanchori of the Anglican parish church of St. Peter's Bissel in Kajiado in Kenya says that the Christian teaching in many mainline Protestant churches is very general and does not address adequately issues related to spirits. Most church teaching is limited to sermons to the whole congregation on Sundays. The focus is also limited. Christians are told clearly about their Christian faith and taught not to believe in any kinds of spirits and that belief in the spirits is unbiblical, evil and idolatrous.

A few congregations, however, offer more teaching and have succeeded to some extent in enabling Christians to grow in their faith. The Moravian church at Uyole in Mbeya, Tanzania, is a good example of this. It provides classes to Christians twice a week using clear outlines designed to enable every Christian to understand the teaching according to his or her level of biblical knowledge. The purpose is to help Christians to mature in their faith so that they are not disturbed either by the spirits or by psychological problems.

Poor counselling contributes to the problem with spiritism. Many pastors do not learn to understand the root causes of the problems affecting the people who come to them for advice and counselling. They also wait for people to come to them with their problems but are not ready to go to people in their homes. Because they want their cases to be kept confidential, very few Christians who are disturbed by spirits go to their pastor. Pastor Kanchori said that if a Christian is weak (because spirits are disturbing him), a pastor should ask himself why this person is so weak and he should be quick to visit the victim to give pastoral advice and help. Because pastors do not do this, Christians go secretly to local medical specialists and diviners for help.

Pentecostal churches are known for using spiritual conventions and power encounters to teach about spirits. People need to hear in words and see in action (through prayers for healing and deliverance from the spirits) that by his death and resurrection Christ disarmed evil and all its powers and triumphed over them. Then they understand that all who are in Christ Jesus can triumph over them as well (Col 2:13–15). The aim of the events is to win people from traditional beliefs to Christianity and to strengthen Christians whose faith has been weakened because of spirits. People who claim to be tortured by evil spirits are prayed for and those who seem to be possessed by spirits are delivered through prayer in the name of Jesus Christ.

An Anglican pastor explained how he had to cast out spirits from a Christian witchdoctor called Israel. This witchdoctor was using evil powers and charms (*hirizi*) in his work and many people including Christians were going to him for healing. The pastor told him that he was doing evil and must stop so that God would not curse him. The man feared the spirits, but the pastor told him that he would pray for him and cast out the spirits. In addition, the pastor assured him that Christ Jesus would protect him from the spirits. The witchdoctor accepted the pastor's advice, and the pastor prayed for him to be delivered from the spirits. His charms were burned, he suffered no subsequent ill effects and the pastor continues to visit him regularly to strengthen him spiritually.

Not many people who are possessed by the spirits, however, would go for deliverance. The majority of Christians choose to continue following traditional practices than to abandon the spirits as the church teaches them to do because they fear the power of the spirits and do not have assurance about the power of Christ.

As part of their evangelism program, some congregations do have occasional follow-up programmes to strengthen the faith of those who seem to be weakened by the spirits. These churches do door-to-door visits and form small groups for prayer and Bible studying.

The Roman Catholics does not ignore the existence of both good and evil spirits. Few Catholic priests take part in power encounter ministries during which spirits are exorcised, but most help Christians afflicted by evil spirits by giving them pastoral counselling. Ministry by power encounter is not common within Roman Catholic traditions. The counselling ministry, however, has been shown to be less effective than the power encounter. Pastoral counselling on its own is not enough. Christians need pastoral counselling that is accompanied by a power encounter. This has been the major factor in many Christians from the Roman Catholic Church deciding to also go to churches that have ministry by power encounter as well or to go back to the spirits for immediate help.

All these efforts, however, have not been effective in producing a shift of allegiance from reliance on the spirits to reliance on the living Christ.

The churches have failed first because missionaries who brought Christianity to Africa also brought a rationalistic Western world view. When they proclaimed the gospel, they unconsciously did so from the perspective of their culture, which dismissed the African world view. They ignorantly downplayed both the African spirit world and biblical supernatural and mystical elements as foolish and unreal. They dismissed Africans beliefs in the existence of spirits as imagination. They asked African converts to relinquish all of their own beliefs and bow down unthinkingly before the imported system of religious orthodoxy. Recent missionaries, who now come from around the world, tend to do the same thing.

Missionaries have also failed to learn the values of African Christians. When they developed a strong orientation in churches toward analyzing the Christian message and systematizing its doctrine, they took an approach that was irrelevant to the African world. For African Christians the ability of Christianity to solve the problems of daily life is what is most relevant. They want a faith that helps them with their traditional concerns about supernatural powers, rather than a faith that helps them learn theological truth and fact. African Christians also want to continue upholding traditional values especially those related to families.

Unfortunately, missionaries' misconceptions about African traditional beliefs and practices have been passed on to the African church leaders like pastors, bishops and so on. Generations of African church officials had received their theological training in Western theological institutions. Protestant pastors and local church leaders in many African countries have been trained in a Western style and have not contextualised biblical teaching in relation to the African world view and traditional values. As a result, often much emphasis is placed on faith in Christ as saviour from sin but little on prayer and practical assistance to help people overcome the harassments of the spirit world. Many pastors are satisfied with this because they think people need to know about salvation from sin and nothing else. Thus, they do not give Christ Jesus is enough space to work in power among people.

Following the Second Vatican Council, which encouraged respectful dialogue between the Roman Catholic Church and followers of African traditional beliefs, the Roman Catholic Church has approached traditional beliefs and practices, including the cult of the spirits, from an anthropological point of view. It is examining itself to find what it has or has not done to reach the hearts of African Christians and of the followers of traditional religions. Bishop Justin Samba of Musoma admits, 'The religion is part and parcel of the life of people in Africa … African Traditional Religion, despite many years of negative propaganda against it by Christians, is still alive and remains the religious and cultural context from which most Christians in Africa come, and in which many of them still live to great extent' (Isizoh 2001b). The Catholic church has not accommodated aspects of traditional religious practices into its practice, though it has started investigating the possibility of incorporating some traditional values. Some priests and theologians are involved informally in dialogue with leaders and followers of African traditional religions.

One group, the African Independent Churches, has respected certain elements of traditional religious practices. Many of their practices, like prayer, healing processes, and fortune telling, originate in traditional practices. Traditional religious practitioners are allowed to be members and leaders of these churches and to continue practising their traditional cults in hope that they will change and become true Christians. African Independent Churches are accused by other churches of being syncretistic. Nevertheless, its followers feel more at home in them than in other churches.

Because African Christians still fear the spirits and are not strong in their faith, they need the message of the gospel theologically contextualised to their world view. They need thorough and practical teaching that will assure them that God's help is not as far away as they think, but rather it is immanent and even more sufficient than that of the spirits. This kind of gospel message will enable the church to fully assume her authority and power in Christ and to thoroughly touch the spiritual depth of the religious African person. For the church to make such a shift, it needs to adopt more biblical theological beliefs and pastoral practices. In his letter to the Colossians, Paul dealt with a similar situation and provided teaching that can help the African church.

CHAPTER THREE

The Relevance of the Book of Colossians to the Church in Africa

Paul's letter to the church at Colossae is relevant to the church in Africa south of the Sahara because, like the Christians in Colossae, Christians in Africa have misunderstood the role of Christ and the place of spirits. A study of Paul's teaching and a comparative study of Colossae and Africa reveal how the church in Africa can relevantly address the issue of the spiritual power that threatens the church. In his letter, Paul provides both theological and pastoral assistance to the African church.

Background of Colossae: Cultural and Religious Complexity

Because of its location, Colossae became a cosmopolitan city with diverse religious and cultural elements that eventually competed with Christianity. The city sat on a bank of a meandering river in the Lycus Valley in southeast Asia Minor (modern Turkey). The city had been built on the main road connecting Ephesus and Sardis with the Euphrates to the east. By the New Testament period, people from all parts of the Greek Empire and then the Roman Empire had settled in the Lycus. Two things drew them. The valley's fertility encouraged agricultural activities and Colossae served as a centre for the valley's prosperous wool and weaving industries. The city was a hub of transportation because it was situated on the route between major cities and the river's tributaries provided good communication between cities on the coast and in the interior.

Although Colossae's commercial importance had almost diminished by New Testament times, the city remained multicultural and multi-faith. While no information is available about the number of local cults and the nationalities of people, external sources indicate that a sizeable Jewish population of about 10,000 lived in the city (Schweizer 1982:14).

The Colossian letter provides clear evidence that Gentiles of Greek tradition as well as Jews inhabited Colossae. The author's references to Gnostic terms like 'philosophy' (2:8), 'knowledge' (1:6, 9–10; 2:2–3), cosmic powers and 'authority' (2:10, 15) and 'the elements of the universe' (2:8, 20) authenticate the presence of Gentiles of Greek tradition. Likewise, the mentioning of Judaic terms in the letter like 'circumcision and uncircumcision' (2:11–13; 3:11), 'calendar piety,' and the 'observance of the Sabbath' (2:16) and to food and purity rules (2:16, 21) indicates that ethnic Jews and Jewish proselytes lived in Colossae (1996:34).

As is the case in Africa, significant levels of religious syncretism existed in the Roman Empire, especially in the Hellenistic world. In the absence of any widely recognised religion, people experimented. They were trying to create new religions from existing religions to provide richer and more satisfying teaching than the other religions offered. Consequently, people tended to borrow valuable elements from cult to cult (Scott 1936:9). Because of its religious and cultural diversity, Colossae, like other major cities in the Lycus Valley, had its share of new religious systems that represented a mixture of religious ideas and different cults. Those new cults were a mix of religions and philosophical ideas from Greece, the Near East, and Rome and of Judaism (Wright 1986:22).

Many scholars identify the teaching in Colossae as 'the Colossian heresy.' Other scholars prefer to call it 'the Colossian philosophy' to avoid making a judgement because the teachers of the new religion sincerely intended to provide good and richer teaching, although the outcome was error (Dunn 1996:25). The purpose of the philosophy was to assure people of their security and blessing here on earth and the ascension of their souls to the upper world when they died.

The Colossian Philosophy and Spiritual Powers

Theologians do not agree on the nature of the false teachings in Colossae because of the limited historical knowledge available and because the Colossian epistle does not address the false teaching in a systematic way. Some theologians suggest the teaching was developed from a pagan cult; others suggest it was based on forms of sectarian Judaism; and still others suggest that it blended the two (Wright 1986:23). In discussing the Colossian philosophy, Paul did not try to separate the Jewish elements from those that were Gnostic or pagan. He 'passes backwards and forwards from the one to the other in such a way as to show that they are only parts of one complex whole' (Lightfoot 1961:75).

However, a closer examination of the language of Colossians provides invaluable clues regarding the nature of the Colossian philosophy. It blended Judaism and Gnostic traditions and beliefs from local cults, magic, and astrology. Teachers of the philosophy called on adherents to observe the demands of the Jewish code, like the rules on food, festivals, the Sabbath, and unclean things. They also stressed the importance of following a variety of mystery rites and ascetic disciplines; they required followers to worship angels and astral bodies.

The main teaching of the Colossian philosophy, as indicated in Colossians 1:16; 2:8, 15, 18, 20 was about *stoicheia*. Theologians differ on the meaning of the term, suggesting two possibilities: one is that it means elemental or fundamental principles (2:8, 20); another is that it means cosmic or spiritual forces (1:16; 2:15, 18).

As Ferdinando says, the first group of theologians identify stoicheia as elemental or fundamental principles. He says that, in the Colossian context, they were elementary teachings that some Judaistic or pagan ritualists imposed on the church (1999:411–416). The teaching was materialistic, was bound up with this world alone and was contrary to the freedom in the Spirit. As elemental principles, stoicheia were also legalistic and contrary to Christ. As in Galatia, some Jewish teachers accommodated Jewish rules and regulations in the teachings of the Colossian church. They wanted Christians to continue observing the basic principles of Jewish rites and of pagan rules, such as ascetic practices, alongside their Christian faith. (Col 2:20). 'It was to these principles that the Galatians and Colossians were in danger of returning' (Ferdinando 1999:411–412).

The second group of theologians say that stoicheia were cosmic or spiritual powers. The stoicheia, according to Patzia (1990:5), 'were the basic or fundamental principles of knowledge and creation, thus making up the totality of the world.' However, under the influence of Hellenistic syncretism, especially during Paul's time, these first principles were elevated to the status of spirits, or were personified as cosmic rulers Along with all the other astral bodies in the universe like the stars, the sun, the moon and the planets, they were divinised as powers and were worshipped.

Arnold has made similar suggestions concerning the meaning of stoicheia. He says that the term stands either for the spirits governing the physical elements like the sun, the moon, the planets and the stars, or that it refers to the spirits as the heavenly powers comprising the fullness of things. The term may also simply stand for evil angels and demons or for the basic principles common to all religions, the domain of Jewish ritual and worship, and intermediaries, such as Jewish law or pagan deities, that stand between God and humanity.

In addition, O'Brien says that the term stoicheia is associated with spirits and that these spirits were believed to have power to control entry into God's presence. They were presented by false teachers as the local presiding deities and associated gods, who controlled and ruled the lives of people. Thus, in the context of Colossians 2:8, the basic principles of this world were the spirits who rivalled Christ, the sole mediator (O'Brien 1987:132). In comparing the situation in Colossae with that in Africa south of the Sahara, this book, this book identifies stoicheia as spirits.

According to some scholars, the beliefs about angels may have been based on a form of Judaism in Phrygia. This type of Judaism may have emerged because of two major influences, namely Hellenism and other literature. Some synagogues in Phrygia seemed to not only have been exposed to the influences of Hellenistic speculation, but also to have assimilated religious beliefs and practices.

The religious life and literature of non-Jewish people in Asia Minor was full of terms related to angels. 'People in the area commonly called upon (angels)—regardless of primary religious orientation— for protection and help' (Arnolds 1996:86). Thus, the folk Judaism of Colossae may have borrowed from this Hellenistic emphasis. The focus was on angels instead of on God. In this form of Judaism, angels were regarded as the divine mediators between God and human beings; their task was to protect people and their properties from various forms of evil and help them with the affairs of daily life.

The Jewish apocalyptic literature of the inter-testamental period had held angels in high regard as intercessors between God and human beings. In the book of 1Enoch 69, it is clear that angels, as mediators, were more involved in the daily affairs of the people of God than God himself was. In addition, in 1 Enoch 7:1–8:3 the fallen angel teaches people about practices like magic medicine, incantation and astrology. The impact is seen during the Greco-Roman period, when devoted Jews like the soldiers of Judas Maccabeus (2 Macc 13:32–45) wore amulets for protection against enemies, accidents, illness and demons. Also, although worshipped God in the Judaism of the inter-testamental period, they gave increasing prominence to angels. They believed angels were closely associated with heavenly powers.

The Influence of Spiritual Powers in Colossae

The followers of the Colossian philosophy assumed spiritual powers were important in two ways: to mediate with God and to protect people from evil spirits. In their role as mediators, the spirits were thought to act as a go-between between human beings and the one high God. They were also seen as rulers of the cosmic spheres and as the source of the wisdom and secret knowledge needed for salvation. To benefit from the spirits, people had to venerate the spirits. They had to participate in doctrinal instruction, ritual, prophecy, sacramental initiation and self-discovery, before the spirits could grant them the wisdom and knowledge that would mysteriously unite their soul with God. People also had to adopt ascetic practices because they were helpful in keeping people free from contamination or pollution by matter.

In their role as guardians, cosmic spirits were thought to have powers to which people could appeal for protection and deliverance from the control of evil spiritual powers. It was believed that two classes of supernatural powers surrounded people: good spiritual powers and hostile spiritual powers. 'His safety was to be bound in the conciliation of the friendly powers by means of offering, sacred rites, spells and talismans, so that they would protect him against the opposing demons' (Scott 1936:49).

It was also important for a person to seek the help and protection of friendly spiritual powers through the rigorous disciplines of self-denial, such as fasting, abuse of the body and other ascetic practices (Arnold 1996:311). In this regard, people in Colossae and the regions around gave high respect to angels because they believed that angels played a more significant role than other spiritual powers in their religious lives. Angels had special powers to control the heavenly realm and man's access to God's presence. It was, therefore, necessary for people to seek the help of angels in attaining esoteric knowledge for reaching the divine presence and for gaining the fullness of salvation. People also needed the help of angels in the affairs of daily life. People seeking the special favour of the angels had to carry out certain rituals. As O'Brien writes,

> *In Colossian false teaching these angels were to be placated by keeping strict legal observance. The breaking of the law incurred their displeasure and brought the lawbreaker into debt and bondage to them (Col 2:12–15). These angels … were not only elemental beings but also*

> *dominant ones as well as principalities and intermediaries between heaven and earth … Apparently they were thought to control the lines of communication between God and man. All this was presented as a form of advanced teaching for the spiritual elite (O'Brien 1987:xxxiii).*

The Influence of Spiritual Powers in the Colossian Church

Because of the Colossian philosophy, a new teaching emerged within the Christian community in Colossae as advocates of the philosophy mixed their Christian faith with aspects of Phrygian religions and Gnostic–Judaism. References like Colossians 2:4, 8, 9, 21, 23 suggest that the Colossian congregation was influenced by a Gnostic–Jewish form of piety. This had two possible outcomes for the church.

First, because Colossae was still open to every kind of strange religion, false teachers welcomed Christianity for their own benefit and, perhaps, some of them became Christians. They seem to have tried to fit fragments of the Christian message into their philosophy. In attempting this, they created a teaching that was superficially attractive (Col 2:4, 23), but that tended to undermine the gospel of Christ (Bruce 1988:98). They taught that in his manhood, Jesus represented God, but in some imperfect manner and so to gain full salvation a person had to observe rituals to supplement the incompleteness of Christ's saving power and help (O'Brien 1987:133).This belief developed because of the Gnostic understanding that God, as pure spirit, could not have direct contact with matter, which was seen as evil. This also disqualified Jesus from being the God-man and from being sufficient as our mediator. Rather Jesus was seen as just one mediator in a series of intermediaries between heaven and earth.

This Colossian philosophy held that for Jesus to mediate effectively between people and God, who was seen as remote and inaccessible, it was important for him to experience the difficulties of being human by having direct contact with matter. Thus, the death and resurrection of Jesus had no special significance for the salvation of people because it was the death and resurrection of one among the many angels-spirits (intermediaries between the one high God and the people on earth).

Second, it seems likely that Christians were vulnerable to continued syncretism. Paul points out that even though they were united with Christ in their baptism (Col 2:12), believers were still subject to the influence of moral evil and spiritual powers (Col 2:20). Prior to their conversion, both the Gentiles, the majority, and Jews, the minority, who formed the church, might have been followers of the cults of local deities or been influenced by the surrounding false teaching and practices. So these Christians may have continued to draw on those experiences as a partial basis for their claim of wisdom and understanding. Also, becoming Christians did not mean that those who had sincere faith in Christ had automatically become immune to the influence of their world views and traditional religious practices. Arnold writes:

> *Many did not and continued to struggle especially with fear over the impact and potential impact the hostile powers could have on their day to day lives. They faced a great temptation to resort to the mechanism for dealing with these supernatural powers that they had depended on for their entire lives (1996:311).*

As noted earlier, false teachers held that integrating mystery rites in church practices was important for supplementing Christ's saving powers and for letting Christians gain the additional knowledge and wisdom that would help them to deal with invisible hostile powers and spirits.

These false teachers also claimed that two important apostolic teachings were false. One was the claims that Jesus was powerful enough to free people from moral evil and supernatural powers. The other was that he had fully disclosed God's redemptive plan through his death and resurrection.

Thus, Colossian believers wanted to establish a Christian mystery initiation rite. In this rite, deities and powers like angels would be honoured along with Jesus Christ, festivals held and sacrifices of purification, offerings, and initiations performed. The reconciling work of Christ would be supplemented by ascetic discipline. The false teachers taught that human beings who belonged to the lower material world needed to be secured against hostile powers imprisoned in the lower material world. After they had freed themselves from the polluted matter through ascetic discipline, Jesus Christ could then perfectly redeem them from moral evil.

A Comparison of Traditional World Views in Africa and Colossae

Although the background of and emphasis in the Colossian philosophy and in the traditional religions in Africa differ, particularly in the area of ancestors and spirits, many similarities exist between the two. As a result, the church in African can learn from Paul's instructions to the Colossians how to deal relevantly with the issue of the spirits, both theologically and practically.

Prior to their conversion to Christianity, both Colossians and Africans followed local religions. The Colossian Christians might have followed Phrygian religions, or Gnostic-Judaism, or been influenced by other false teachings. Many of African Christians have either followed traditional religions or were brought up in an environment where traditional religious practices were popular.

Colossians Christians continued to appeal to their past visionary experiences and spiritual powers for security and prosperity. African Christians, too, have not fully shifted from the traditional religious practices to Christ, and still appeal to spirits for assurance of security and abundant life.

Moreover, after becoming Christians, the Colossians continued to live in an area where local deities and cults were still active. This meant that even those with sincere faith faced a great temptation to resort to older mechanisms for dealing with the supernatural powers they had depended on for their entire lives (Arnold 1996:311). Like the Colossians, African Christians are not immune to the influence of the world views and traditional religious practices prevalent in their areas.

Syncretism was an issue in the Colossian church. The false teachers integrated mysterious rites of local cults into church practices, honouring deities and spiritual powers along with Christ. This problem also exists in West Africa, Central Africa, Southern Africa, and in the large cities of East Africa, like Nairobi and Dar-es-Salaam, where churches have integrated practices associated with the spirits and witchcraft of local cults into Christianity. They do this to accumulate wealth. Under the umbrella of the name of Christ, leaders of these churches magically cast out demons and other evil spirits and heal people of their diseases, and people will pay to receive this kind of ministry.

Likely, the Colossian and African world views are closely related. Though they did so from different perspectives, people from both areas viewed the universe as being governed by spiritual powers. The Colossians viewed the cosmic spheres as being inhabited and ruled by both good and bad elemental forces. According to the Colossian philosophy, these two classes of spiritual powers had great influence on people. Africans see their whole cosmos as being inhabited and controlled by good and evil supernatural powers, namely the ancestral spirits and other spirits. Africans, too, believe that the spirits have both positive and negative influences on lives of individuals and of the community.

Religiously, both the Colossians and Africans regarded the spirits as mediators between God and human beings. According to the traditional teachings in Colossae, spirits were rulers of cosmic spheres and were intermediaries between earth and heaven. They had the power to control the communication between God and people and to unite the souls of people with God. That meant people had to venerate them and observe certain ritual instructions to gain the spirits' favour and to avoid punishment.

Africans believe that the spirits, particularly the ancestral spirits, stand between God and people on earth. Their main function is bridge communication between God and the people for reconciliation and for the constant flow of God's blessing. Therefore, like the Colossians, Africans are obliged to offer sacrifices and to perform religious rituals to maintain good relationships with the spirits.

The Colossians, as do Africans today, thought the spiritual powers had a great impact as far as life and its completeness was concerned. According to the Colossian philosophy, good spiritual powers enabled a person to gain material blessings and protection against the destructive evil spiritual powers. The prosperity of a person was completely in the hands of the cosmic powers. Similarly, Africans believe that the spirits, particularly the good ones, have the power to cause individuals and the whole community to prosper materially and to guarantee security and protection. As discussed earlier, Africans also believe that spirits have the power to bring curses and misfortunes. Thus, like the Colossians, Africans see the need to have good relationships with the spirits.

Misconceptions about Christ lay at the root of the problem in Colossae and still do in Africa. According to Acts 19:10, signs and wonders performed in the name of Jesus accompanied the proclamation of the apostolic gospel in Asia Minor, where Colossae was situated. Yet some Colossian Christians doubted Christ's saving power (Col 2:6–8) and ability to protect them. Similarly, after generations of Christianity in Africa, African Christians hold that Christ's power is not sufficiently available to help them in their daily lives and to protect them against the spirits. A close look at Colossians reveals that people do not need to turn to spirits to supplement Christ's power to meet their needs.

CHAPTER FOUR

Christ and Spiritual Powers: A Detailed Study

Although the major problem the church in Africa is not related to theology to the same extent that is was in Colossae, the message of Colossians is relevant to the African church. It shows that the false teaching was diminishing the person of Jesus and his role in relation to the church and creation. Understanding this, and the true power of Christ, will help the church in Africa to realize how it can deal with spiritual powers in the African context and help African Christians deal with their fear of spirits.

A Contextual Theological Response to the Religious Situation

Because the church in Colossae was compromising Christianity with the teachings of Colossian philosophers, Christians were in danger of falling away from the truth of the gospel they had received through apostolic tradition (Col 1:6). Meeting the false teachers on their own ground, Paul wrote the Colossian epistle to correct false teachings and to reassure the Christians of the truth of the Gospel of Christ, which they had received. He also wanted to reassure Christians of the truth of the gospel of Jesus Christ. Paul's concern in the book of Colossians, therefore, was both theological and practical.

The Adequacy of Jesus Christ as Saviour

Before dealing with theological issues, Paul began his letter with pastoral words of encouragement, commendation and assurance. He praised the believers for their readiness to activate the teaching of the gospel they received from Epaphras in their lives, saying that the faith and love they had was clear indication of this (Col 1:3–8). Paul assured them that, even though he was not with them, he prayed for them always. He prayed that they might bear more fruits in every good work and continue being filled with the knowledge of God's will. He prayed that with that knowledge they could grow in their faith, 'being strengthened with all power according to God's glorious might so that' they, as Christians, could 'have great endurance and patience,' especially in times of desperation, and (Col 1:9–12).

The apostle also wanted to assure them of the benefits believers receive from God. Through faith in Christ, believers were forgiven their sins, rescued from the dominion of darkness to light and transferred from the slavery of the power of evil to the power of God. They were qualified by God as his children to share his inheritance in his eternal kingdom of light (Col 1:12–14). This kind of assurance was important to Colossian Christians, who feared the unseen forces of darkness.

Then Paul replis to the criticism of the false teachers and of what they have claimed about Christ and the power of the spirits. The apostle first affirms the role of Christ in the Church (Col 1:15–20).and then challenges the Colossians to 'live in him' (Col 2:6) and goes on to refute the Colossian philosophy. To confirm Jesus Christ's role, Paul begins with a powerful statement about Jesus' divine nature. He says that Christ is the exact likeness of God. God, who was unseen, had become visible in the bodily form of Jesus Christ. Jesus does not merely reflect God, but also reveals God to us. As the firstborn over all creation, he is the one who is before everything, and it is by his will and his supreme power that all things on earth and in heaven, including the powers, were created and exist (Col 1:16–17). Also as firstborn, Jesus has all the priority and authority of the firstborn prince in a king's household (Col 1:15).

According to this passage, Christ is identified as Logos (even if the word 'Logos' is not used in the book). As Logos, Jesus is sovereign Lord and superior to the whole universe. He created all things and in him everything visible and invisible, even the powers and principalities, is held together, protected and kept from destruction (Col 1:16–17). According to Hellenistic teaching, Logos was 'the principle of creation, the intermediary between God and the world' (Scott 1936:12). As Logos, Christ must not be regarded as one of the powers because the various ranks of powers are of the created order and their existence depends on him. He is the sovereign Lord, and everything, including the spiritual powers, is subject to his Lordship. As Logos, 'Christ is not just one deity among many, nor is he some kind of angelic mediator figure. He is Lord over all in the same way that Yahweh is Lord over all' (Arnold 1996:258). In mediating between God and the world, Jesus does not require assistance from any other power. There is completeness in him because he is the supreme Lord of all, the Lord who possesses all the fullness of God's power, essence and glory.

In describing the role of Christ, Paul says that Christ is supreme in all things. Paul describes him as 'the head of the body, the Church; he is the beginning and the first-born from among the dead, so that in everything he might have the supremacy' (Col 1:18). Paul says that the fullness of God dwells in Christ, which means that he has all God's attributes. Thus, Christ, who was a man because he was incarnate, is also God. Christ's position has a number of implications for the Church and the world. As the creator of everything, he is the one who enables everything to exist, including various ranks of powers. As the founder and head of the Church, he redeems people who are enslaved by sin and death. By his death on the cross and resurrection, he has defeated sin and death and has become God's salvation to all people on earth. He enables believers to die to sin and rise with him to a new life of righteousness (Rom 6:1–10).

Because the fullness of God dwells in him and because of his death and resurrection, Christ has the power to give life and power to believers if they fully commit themselves to him. He gives them the Holy Spirit to lead them in this new life so that they will not again become slaves of sin (John 14:26; 16:13; Rom 8:1–8). In Colossians 1: 21–22, Paul says that because of Christ's death humans and God have been reconciled and so humans can be presented holy before God. Christ is the good shepherd to Christians. With his supreme power, he provides believers with their day to day needs whenever they pray to God in his name (Matt 7:7–11; Mark 11:24; John 11:13–14). He also protects them from all dangers like accidents, illnesses and other misfortunes, (John 10:1–13) including those caused by evil spirits (Arnold 1999:38–39).

Paul refutes several misconceptions that existed in the Colossian church (Col 1:15–23). Believing that matter is evil, the false teachers argued that God could not have come down to earth as a true human being in bodily form. To correct the misconception, Paul makes the point that Christ is the image of the invisible God and is God (Col 1:15–17) and died on the cross as a human being (Col 1:18, 20, 22).

False teachers held that Christ was not the unique Son of God, but rather one of many intermediaries between God and people. Paul's claim that Jesus existed before anything else as the firstborn over all creation is the answer to that (Col 1:15).

Moreover, false teachers refused to believe in Christ as the only source of salvation, insisting that in addition to faith in Christ (as one of many intermediaries) people could find God through secret knowledge and legalistic rituals. Paul had to teach clearly that salvation is found in Christ

Jesus alone because he alone, by his death and resurrection, has the power to defeat evil and all its powers and to redeem people who are enslaved by it (Col 1:20–23).

The notion of Christ's reconciliation of all things (Col 1:20) presupposes his supremacy over spiritual powers. Ferdinando suggests that the 'powers and authorities' referred to in Colossians 2:14–15 are evil spiritual beings related to Satan, which were disarmed of their power by Christ on the cross. Because of Christ, the sin that enslaved people and separated them from God is defeated and the reconciliation between God and all things, including sinful people, is established (Col 1:20–22). By his death and resurrection, Jesus Christ became the Lord of reconciliation so there is redemption and forgiveness of sin for those who believe and remain in him (Col 1:23). An essential connection exists between forgiveness of sins and victory over the powers and principalities. In that they have individually received forgiveness for their sins, people are freed from bondage to the powers (Col 1:13–23). In Christ, God removes sins and strips the powers (Ferdinando 1999:293).

In commenting on Colossians 1:20, Ferdinando is right in suggesting that the defeat of the powers marks the beginning of the era of universal reconciliation. He asserts that the death and resurrection of Jesus Christ broke the authority of the powers over humanity and that, since their power is neutralised, the powers can no longer enslave people. The death and resurrection of Jesus Christ has ended the powers' defiance of his sovereignty. The universe has been reconciled to God and has been brought back into its divinely created and determined order under the headship of Christ. It is now possible for believers to enjoy the benefits of the universe without any fear of evil powers, provided the believers persevere in the Christian faith.

Paul had a very practical purpose in teaching about Christ's role. He wanted the Colossians to realize that having received a new life in Christ, they needed to live 'rooted in Christ,' so they could mature in their faith and be built up and strengthened in Christ. (Col 2:6–8). Paul says he doesn't want anyone to 'delude [them] through beguiling speech' (Col 2:4). He even orders them ('see to it') to not let themselves be taken 'prey' by 'hollow and deceptive philosophy, which depends on human tradition and the basic principles of this world' (*stoicheia tou kosmou*) (Col 2:8). If they allow false teaching to penetrate the church and their lives, they would remain immature in their Christian faith and evil powers would continue to threaten them. They needed to follow apostolic gospel teaching because Christ's power is enough to save believers from sin and protect them from any attack of evil power.

Before he deals with some of the problem practices, Paul reminds them of their position in Christ. He takes them step-by-step through the process that has given them the new relationship with God that allows them to participate solidly in Christ's victory over evil powers. In Col 2: 9–14, Paul returns to the concept of fullness in Christ. He says that the totality of God with all his powers and attributes is fully present in Christ's human body. God is all powerful and the one who causes every power and authority to exist. Christ is the Son of God and so the absolutely authentic representation of God in bodily form here on earth. He is, therefore, the head over every power and authority, because he is their creator and sustainer (Col 1:16–17). The evil powers are also subjected to his authority. By his death on the cross Christ has conquered and disarmed the evil powers (Eph 6:12) and has rescued believers from their dominion. For through baptism, which is the inward circumcision of their bodies in their hearts, they were also given the fullness of Christ by God. Believers have had their sinful natures put to death by God. They became fully united with Christ and superior to every power and authority (Col 2:10), including the evil ones.

The exaltation of Christ was the exaltation of Christians. They fully shared in Christ's enthronement and exaltation both then and in the future in heaven (Col 2:12; 3:4). They become alive in righteousness and solidly participate in Jesus' victory over death, over evil powers and over the spiritual and eternal realm in which Christ has been exalted and enthroned (Col 2:12, 13; 3:1). Colossians Christians have now died with Christ to the basic principles of this world, namely Jewish-Gnostic rules (Col 2:13–15). They are raised with him to a new life of righteousness, are completely surrounded by his saving power on earth and are assured of appearing with Christ in glory (3:1–4). Another reason they are alive is that God has 'disarmed the principalities and powers' and 'triumphed over them' (Col 2:15). Later, Paul writes, 'If with Christ you have died to the elemental spirits of the universe, why do you live as if you still belonged to the world (Col 2:20). Here, Paul addresses one of false teachings in the Colossian philosophy—the alleged power of the spirits. Ferdinando says

> *The concern is to underline the subjection of the enemies of Christ's people to Christ himself, and so to assure the readers that the powers are not in control and believers are not in debt or bondage to them and do not need to placate them. Christ's present reign is thus the guarantee of final salvation not withstanding the powers' continuing animosity (1999:295).*

Paul is also careful to warn the Colossians that, although Christ defeated the evil powers on the cross, he did not destroy them (Col 2:15). Rather, Paul says, God conquered them. Evil powers still exist and work against people and their interests (cf. Rom. 8:38, 39), but are powerless to affect those who live under the lordship of Jesus. Christians who are genuinely submitted to the lordship of Christ can not be harmed by evil powers. Colossian Christians, therefore, were to remain firmly anchored to Christ so that they could be safe from the influence of evil powers.

This is not only a relevant response to the false teachers' criticism of the gospel, but also is an important response to Colossian Christians who needed to be reassured of the complete adequacy of Jesus for their strength and security. Paul insists that Christians do not need to seek for additional help, 'namely that which the Colossian philosophy offers, in realizing their salvation and for coping with the onslaught of the powers.' Rather,

> *[T]hey have every reason for thanksgiving, for they have been relocated into the kingdom of their loving and*

> *powerful Lord. Within this dominion, they have access to an abundant supply of divine power to protect them from the continuing and compelling influence of the evil 'powers' and to strengthen them to resist the encroaching influence of the burgeoning philosophy (Arnold 1996:270).*

Paul then shows the Colossians that they did not need to supplement Christ's saving power by combining their Christian faith with the commands and traditions the false teachers urged them to follow. False teachers demanded that Christians observe rules and regulations, alongside Christianity, because Christ's power was not enough to save them from moral evil, was not able to unite their souls with God and was not able to free and protect believers from the influence of destructive powers. Paul tells them not to let anyone judge them by what they eat or drink, Col 2:16), or they how thy observe festivals and keep the Sabbath. These Jewish rites were 'a shadow' (Col 2:17), not the real thing, but a shadow because they symbolically depicted the coming of Christ who fulfilled God's salvation plan.

The Christians were not to be influenced by those who said promoted false humility or worshipping angels (Col 2:18). Paul said that these teachers had lost contact with Christ (Col 2:19). It can be assumed that the good spiritual forces and angels, whom the Colossians believed they had to placate, were like the other angels and spiritual beings mentioned in the Bible as being created by Christ for various purposes. Angels served as God's messengers to the people (Heb 1:1, 2, 14) and some were assigned by

God to watch over his people (Ps 34:7; Dan 6:22; Matt 18:10). Their role continues, as we read in Heb 13:1–2. Biblical angels operate, under the command of Christ (Matt 24:31; Rev 22:16), as his servant to Christ's people. Apart from this role, angels have no greater importance on human beings. Christ has replaced the roles the Colossians think angels play. As well, the angels would not have operated at the direction of humans who sought their favour because they are responsible to God.

To summarize the book of Colossians, Paul wants the Colossian Christians to understand that they did not need to look beyond Jesus for their spiritual wisdom and knowledge, nor did they need to supplement his power to have fullness of life. Colossian Christians were to remain firmly anchored to Christ so that they can be safe from the influence of evil powers (Col 1:13), for in Christ there is fullness of life and completeness of salvation (Col 1: 20). By following the teachings of the Colossian philosophy, the Colossians would be acknowledging not only that evil powers had authority over them, but also they could not trust the saving power they had received through faith in Christ. Christ alone, not angels and other spiritual powers, is the source of wisdom and knowledge for salvation. Moreover, Jesus Christ has defeated death, evil and all hostile powers. Colossian Christians had to focus their mind on pursuing everything associated with Jesus and Him only because all they needed in terms of their spirituality and security could be found in Jesus (Col 2:10). Once the church in Africa understands Paul's teaching in Colossians, its next step is to apply it theologically and pastorally.

CHAPTER FIVE

Theological and Pastoral Implications of Colossians for the Church in Africa

Paul's message to the Colossians on the sufficiency of Christ's power is what many in the African church need to hear and which church leaders need to use. His letter provides the church in Africa with the theological foundation to show Christians that they lack nothing in their relationship with Jesus Christ and so do not have to supplement Christ's power with spiritism. Because of the parallels between Colossae and African south of the Sahara, Paul's teaching is applicable to African religious and cultural beliefs. And Paul's example of applying the gospel to the local situation shows how the gospel can be contextualized. Similarly, some churches in Africa have found biblical ways to contextualize this truth and so provide good pastoral care. As their examples show, churches can find ways to minister effectively to Africans.

Theological Implications: Contextual Approach of Colossians in the African Perspective

The major theological problem that the church in Africa faces is a limited understanding of the extent of Christ's saving power. As discussed earlier, while African Christians accept that Christ will provide them with a way to heaven, many do not adequately experience his immanent power in their day to day lives. The impact is compounded because many Africans psychologically remain under the dominion of spirits when they become Christians. The church needs to address this directly by providing contextual biblical teaching to enable Christians to appreciate the relevance and sufficiency of God's salvation through Christ. The teaching must assure people that through faith in Christ they are completely saved from sin and have received the power that frees them from the harassment of the spirit world and that helps them to solve their daily problems.

Paul addressed the same issues in his letter to the Colossians, which is why his letter is a sound model for the church in Africa. Churches that deny the reality of spiritual powers need to look at Paul's teaching. He acknowledged the reality of their existence and taught the Colossians the truth about them. African Christians need to know that, as Paul explained, Christ is superior to spiritual powers because the powers are created beings, Christ is their creator, and the powers have no power apart from him. Jewish apocalyptic literature of the inter-testamental period teaches that angels were created by God as his messengers. Some angels, however, rebelled against God and formed a group of the fallen angels (1Enoch 7:1–8:3), which operates against God's will. These fallen angels are the evil powers, in the Colossian context, and do not work under Christ. In African context, demons and evil powers like the jinn belong to this group of fallen angels. Humans do not become angels when they die. Many Africans equate the function of non-ancestral spirits, which is chiefly to cause destruction to people, to that of fallen angels,.

Paul says that Christ alone can bring God's full and complete salvation to humankind and that those who believe in him are completely saved and freed from the influence of legalistic teachings and traditional rituals (Col 2:16–19). African Christians also need to know that threats of excommunication or punishment from the spirit realm for failure to observe rules and regulations carry no weight for a Christian whose Lord has full authority over that realm.

Paul's arguments in the book of Colossians counteract the African concept that God keeps his distance from humans and that humans cannot communicate with God directly. Paul helps people clearly understand the importance of the reconciliation people can have with God through Christ Jesus. In Jesus Christ alone, God has fully disclosed himself in bodily form (Col 1:20). Through Jesus Christ, in whom all God's fullness dwells, reconciliation between God and immoral human beings and everything on earth and in heaven has become possible

(Col 1:20). All things are restored to their rightful place under the rightful order from which they broke loose to rebel against God's purpose. With peace and friendship established between God and human beings, people can now have direct access to God (Col 1:21–22). This means that through faith in Christ people can now appeal to God directly for help with their daily needs for difficult problems like illness, infertility and drought, or when the harmony of the social and cosmic order is severely disturbed. God alone, not ancestors and other spiritual powers, can help African Christians in all difficulties to meet their needs and provide them abundantly according to his will (Ps 1:3; 23:5–6; Matt 7:7; John 14:13–14). The Bible assures us those who are in Christ are like a tree planted by streams of water (Ps 1:3) whose leaf does not wither. God provides for their needs abundantly (Ps 23:5–6) on condition that they remain in him and they pray for their needs according to God's will in the name of Jesus (Matt 7:7; John 14:13–14).

Paul's teaching on Jesus' role on the cross as the mediator between God and humans is also relevant for correcting the belief that people can only communicate with the transcendent God by going through the spirits. According to the book of Colossians, Christ alone is the mediator between God and the world. As the only mediator, Jesus has more qualifications than the spirits to act on behalf of humans. As God's only son, he is nearer to God than any other being and is Lord over all in the same way that God is Lord over all. Moreover, by Jesus' death on the cross people are not only permanently reconciled to God, but also they are made co-heirs with Jesus of God's blessings in his kingdom (Col 1:12-14, 20–22). By his resurrection, Jesus, as mediator, guarantees new life here and hereafter to those who believe in him.

Other sections of the Bible show that, despite some claims to the contrary, God forbids people to contact spirits of the dead for any purpose. When Moses and Elijah appeared to Jesus during his transfiguration, God wanted to tell the world, through the disciples who heard his voice, that they do not need to continue obeying the spirits like Moses and Elijah, but rather they should now listen only to Jesus (Luke 9:35). The story of rich man and Lazarus in Luke 16:19–31 reveals to Christians that communication between the living dead and their families here on earth stops after death. Luke says that a great chasm separates the dead and the people on earth. The dead who might want to come to Earth are not able to do so (Luke 16:26.) The story in 1 Samuel 28:14–20 is a strong warning to those who seek help from the spirits instead of from God. After Saul disobeyed God, God was no longer willing to listen to the king. Terrified by the Philistines' army, Saul used occult practices to seek Samuel's help. God was very angry and allowed Samuel to speak to Saul in this unusual case not to provide help, but to condemn him. This story teaches us that God does not want living people to contact the dead for help or guidance.

Paul also addresses the traditional African belief that God, who is morally good, does not like to live close to immoral human beings. He asserts that God and immoral people are reconciled through Christ because the sins of people are forgiven through faith in the work done on the cross by Jesus. Now, in the man Jesus, God is fully present among people. Believers are given complete salvation (or wholeness of life in the context of Africans) in Christ, the head over every power and authority (Col 1:19, 20; 2:9–10). As Turaki says, 'The theology of redemption and reconciliation in the work of Christ addresses the question of cosmic harmony and must be brought to the questions raised in the African context' (Moreau 2002:24).

Christ's power is superior to that of cosmic spirit forces because he is the son of God (Col 1:13) and, thus, the true representation of God's might, power and authority. Because he is the creator, the various ranks of powers, including spirits, are part of the created order and their existence depends entirely on Christ (Col 1:15–17).

Paul also provides an answer to superstition and the fear of magic powers. By his death on the cross Jesus removed sin and disarmed the powers of evil and established his everlasting kingdom of light (Col 1:11–14). At the time of conversion, Christians are transported from the kingdom of darkness, where evil powers enslaved them, to the kingdom of light. Their sins were forgiven and they were permanently freed from the influences of evil powers in their lives. God also permanently protects Christian by his mighty power (Col 1:11–13; 2:11–12). Believers who walk obediently in their Christian faith have nothing to fear from magic and superstition. Christians do not need to continue appealing to ancestors and other spiritual powers. However, Christians who are not serious in their faith will attract harassment from spiritual forces.

With Colossians as such a valuable resource, how can African churches teach Paul's points so the people understand how they apply to them? How can the churches contextualize this biblical teaching so Christians avail themselves of the power of Jesus in their lives and thus overcome the temptation to return to the spirits?

Pastoral Implications of Contextual Approach to Colossians in the African Perspective

African churches can enable their congregations to understand the power of the gospel by taking two approaches to contextualization. One is to emphasis how the gospel addresses values and issues that are most important to African Christians. The other is to use methods for worship and teaching that are culturally meaningful. Taber was right to say,

> *Theology must be done out of pastoral concern, with the well-being of the person in view. It is not a detached, abstract exercise, but a determined effort to use particular tools to help Christians grow and help non-Christians to come to Christ. The theology must be adapted to people in such a way that they may not only easily understand Christian doctrine, but also be impelled to live the divine mysteries (Taber 1978:63–64).*

For the African church, contextualization will mean developing thoroughly biblical and authentically African Christian teachings and practices that uphold the good values found in traditional religious practices. By so doing, the church will appropriately address topics that are real to the people in their localities, such as the issue of ancestors and other spirits. Richard Gehman, a missionary in Kenya for nearly twenty years church, makes the case for finding points of contact that are meaningful to people. Having done thorough research among the Akamba people on Kenya, Gehman says that that point of contact is found primarily within the people themselves and, secondarily, within various elements of African traditional religion. (2002:265). He is very clear on this point:

> *Mission should demonstrate sympathy towards the animist. It should esteem the heathen's faith as a religion. It should rejoice in every element of truth and goodness found among the animists. Patience is required. Many evil customs exist to meet greater evil in the social life of the people and it is dangerous to displace them until you have given a substitute, which they can accept intelligently … African traditional religion presents a certain points of contact for the preaching of the gospel (2002:266).*

However, contextualizing African traditional values must be done carefully. Gehman says the continuity of these values must be biblically properly measurable to avoid syncretism. He does not give any example of continuity of African traditional values in the church, but he gives examples of how to avoid syncretism. He says that it is syncretism to allow songs with biblical content to be sung to the chant and traditional drumbeat that were used for inducing spirit possession. Also, syncretism occurs when the church retains elements of magic and divination by equating the work of the ancestral spirits with the work of the Holy Spirit and mingling the Holy Spirit with traditional spirits.

In May 1996, Bishop Godfrey Mdimi Mhogolo of the Anglican Church of Tanzania in Diocese of Central Tanganyika in Dodoma discussed the need to integrate good traditional values in the practice of the church, during an address to the diocesan general council meeting. The Bishop said that traditional religious practices permeate all aspects of life of an African person. Thus, to claim this person for Christ, the church needs to enculturate the gospel into the very fabric of each African society.

The church could address a great many traditional values, but two of the most important are the role of the ancestors and the influence of spirits. In his role as mediator between God and humans, Christ Jesus does not negate the responsibility that elders, including Christians, have for their families and communities. Nor does he negate the importance of respecting older family members. Ancestors are the authentic guardians of moral orders of customs in the society and their presence maintains a harmonious life of love, unity, peace and prosperity among people. Honouring parents and the elderly in the community is right and biblical (Lev 19:32). The Bible says clearly that people should submit to the elderly, that they should carefully consider their advice and that they should obey them at all times. By doing so, in some way, they are showing reverence to God himself (Exod 20:12; Prov 1:8).

So the church needs to find biblical ways to support strong families. Some African churches have addressed this need, and, in the process, provided meaningful pastoral care by developing Christian ways of blessing families, showing honour to elders and celebrating rites of passage.

Bishop Jeremiah Taama of the Anglican Church of Kenya in the diocese of Kajiado, gives a good example of the continuity of Maasai religious values in the church. He says that, traditionally, the senior elders of the family blessed members of their family using an ox-tail hair to sprinkle the water of blessings from a locally made bowl. Such practice can be Christianized so that a priest can bless Christians in the church and in their houses by sprinkling them with water using an ox tail. The priests can bless even Maasai farms and livestock in that way. Many pastors both in Kenya and Tanzania supported this idea.

During a discussion about the role of senior leaders in families at the diocesan general council meeting mentioned earlier, Bishop Godfrey Mdimi Mhogolo rightly said that the concept of some type of extended family is at the core of most African societies. This concept serves many useful functions and it is generally held together by ancestral beliefs and rituals. Senior leaders of the families have a mediatory connection with the ancestors and God to ensure the protection of the family against disease and other calamities. The church, therefore, must not take over the role of the heads of families, but should maintain it by allowing the already baptised heads of families to continue with their headship role. As heads of their Christian families, they will do well in leading, teaching and instructing, and blessing their families according to Christian moral principles, and they will do it more successful than church elders and pastors do. Congregations could have a rota or programs that would allow each family under their heads to lead various activities in the church such as services, singing and preaching. According to Bishop Mhogolo, this is how people can feel the church is theirs rather than foreign to them.

Similarly, Rev. Joseph Kanchori Ailo of Kajiado in Kenya said that traditional values that are good could be Christianized. He said that elders of Maasai families are the ones responsible for teaching their youngsters. But the pastors have taken the role of these elders and cannot provide adequate teachings because of the numbers of people in a parish. As an alternative, Kanchori favours following the traditional system, which gives full responsibility to elders of families to equip their youngsters with teachings. He wants these elders to be acquainted with contextualised biblical Christian knowledge to teach their youngsters.

Instead of adopting foreign rituals that make people feel alienated in their own churches, the church in Africa should start adapting indigenous rituals to satisfy, in a Christian manner, the emotional needs of African Christians. Some Christians and pastors have suggested that rituals that structure and make life meaningful should be Christianized. This includes rituals around birth, passage to adulthood, marriage, death, and public crises, such as drought and plagues of insects. There are rituals for reconciliation, for cleansing from abominations such as incest, and for following the agricultural cycles of seeding, hoeing and harvesting. This would make the gospel meaningful in everyday life.

Christians can play an important part in coming-of-age rituals. Rev. Joseph Kanchori Ailo wants the camps for the circumcised Maasai boys to be revived and the teaching traditionally provided to be Christianized. At the moment, according to Kanchori, the church in Kenya discourages both the camps and the teachings. Traditionally, after they were circumcised, the boys camped for a month outside their family residential areas so they could learn traditional teachings. But now boys are kept at home. This is a big mistake, and Kanchori believes that reintroducing the camps and providing Christian teachings will enhance the church's ability to be rooted in the traditional life of the Maasai.

Rev. Isaiah Chambala, who was rural dean of Kibaya deanery in the Anglican Diocese of Mount Kilimanjaro in Tanzania before his transfer to Munguishi Christian Training Centre, described another way to Christianize coming-of-age rituals. While a dean, he visited a church where the evangelist in charge of the church told him that a family was preparation to circumcise their boys. Normally, boys would be required to drink a medicine and to wear something on their necks as a symbol of the presence of family ancestral spirits. This is to prevent the 'evil eye' from harming the boys when circumcision is taking place. Rev. Chamballa asked the elders of the family to allow him to conduct a service of circumcision. Chamballa prayed for the boys and made a wooden cross to hang at the entrance door of the circumcision camp. The cross was a sign of the presence of the power of Jesus Christ in that ceremony and everybody, including the boys, were to enter the camp through that door. He then assured them that the power of Christ is with the boys and the evil eyes of people will not harm them so they did not need to drink local medicine or wear any ancestor symbol. According to Chamballa, the circumcision ceremony went very well because the boys did not have any problems. Now, people in that area want pastors to do the same for their boys. Chamballa suggests another way to help Christians not to be threatened by the fear of destructive spirits; he advises that Christians, especially the newly baptised, wear a small wooden cross of Christ as a sign of being surrounded by his power. In many tribes people either wear something or scratch their bodies as sign of being able to access the power of ancestors that protect them from being attached by destructive spirits.

Christians can find ways to Christianize traditional ways of treating diseases. A Catholic priest in Morogoro has succeeded in doing this by using prayer and ordinary herbs to treat people. Traditionally, specialists like waganga wa kienyeji (local doctors) and magicians provide treatment using local herbs. They use spirits and divination to understand diseases of their customers and to find the right herbs for treatments. The Catholic priest, according to Rev. Canon Yona Masanika of Dodoma in Tanzania, helps many ill people. He prays for the patients in the name of Jesus and insists that God created all those herbs and trees in his garden. He spends enough time with each patient meditating from the Bible on the wonders of God's creation and on God's immeasurable love to human kind in sending Jesus to deal with our sins and problems. Finally, the priest prays for the patients and gives them herbs to drink at home. Rev. Yona Masanika is one of those many patients whose diseases have been cured through this Catholic priest.

Many Christians suggest that traditional ways of prayer and the use of local melodies, tunes and musical equipment should be encouraged in the church. Rev. Naftaly Lemooke and Joseph Kanchori of Kajiado in Kenya said to me that the Maasai people love reciting prayers and singing in their local tunes and language. They find church boring when they use hymn books translated in Swahili to sing and to read prayers from the liturgy. Songs in hymnbooks are translated from old English, American, and German hymns and sung to foreign tunes, and liturgical prayers meet the needs of those for whom they were originally intended. These ministers said that adaptations could be used to give good Christian teaching as long as they are done in the right way and syncretism is avoided. Items for prayer can come from people themselves and must touch all aspects of Maasai life. Maasai always like a prayer that blesses them and their livestock.

The church must also find ways to demonstrate that Christ's power is greater than that of spirits. Then Africans who used to live in traditional beliefs about spirit's power and ability to mediate with God will find Christ a true replacement for the spirits. One suggestion is that when the church proclaims the gospel it does so along with power encounters, such as prayers for healing and deliverance from spirits. Christians familiar with traditional ways need to see and hear that by his death and resurrection Christ disarmed evil and its powers and triumphed over them so that all who are in Christ Jesus can triumph over them as well (Col 2:13–15). For Christians who fear supernatural powers, a power encounter in the name of Jesus is significantly important both for their security and growth in faith.

Similarly, churches need to develop an appropriate ministry for those oppressed by spirits. According to some people, many people who come from areas where spirits have much influence continue to suspect that spirits are attacking them. Whether these attacks are real or not, the church needs to offer help so that Christians with this problem will not be tempted to seek help through divination and spiritism. Ministers should encourage Christians in their local communities to form small teams that can minister to those who have need near them, through prayers and social support.

A spiritual convention organized by all the churches in Dodoma for seven days in October 2004 showed the value of power encounters. The speaker was Rev Dr Peter Youngren, an international preacher from Canada, and I was on the organizing team. The convention was well advertised through posters, tracts, television and radios. All people, including Christians and non-Christians, were invited to come and listen to the good news of Jesus that was to be accompanied by healing and exorcism in the name of Jesus Christ. Normally, when conventions are held that do not inlcude prayers for healing and casting out demons and jinn, a small number of people attend. But thousands of people, both Christians and non-Christians, attended this one, with the number increasing day-by-day as miracles happened. Every day, Dr Peter Youngren encouraged all the Christians in the convention to pray for those with problems, and we thanked God because, by our prayers, Christ did wonders. I know of Christians and non-Christians who had been oppressed by demonic illness for some years who were freed by Jesus. Some Christians from my church had not been attending services for long time because the church was not helping them to overcome their problems. But since then they have become active members. Youngren emphasized that it is Christ who heals people and that prayer for healing is for all times and for all Christians. Christians, therefore, should be in the habit of activating the power of Christ in prayer for healing for ill people and those attacked by demons and other evil power.

These are just a few example of what can be done to contextualize the gospel and to teach a gospel of Christ that is relevant African Christians, that provides continuity with African traditions and that shows that Christ's power is greater than that of spirits. This continuity will let the church meet the religious and emotional needs of Africans; it will help Christians to stop consulting the spirits because they will have truly experienced Christ's saving power in their daily affairs.[0]

With so much that could be done, the church would be wise to focus its efforts and to use Paul's letter to the Colossians as a model for ministry to African Christians.

CHAPTER SIX

Recommendations

As the study of Colossians and the example of churches in Africa have show, the church can find Christian ways to answer the unresolved questions of the African spirit world. It can provide alternatives to westernized Christianity and to African traditional religions. These alternatives would enable Christians to feel at home in the church and, thus, grow in their relationships with Christ Jesus. As the book clearly indicates, African traditional religious values are not necessarily a threat to the gospel; rather they are a challenge to the development of the gospel in the context of the African people. To deal biblically with the issues of spiritual powers, the church in Africa needs to teach the truth about the relationship of spirits and Jesus, to contextualize the gospel so it is meaningful in everyday life, to support pastoral training in Africa and to encourage more research into African traditional religions and biblical ways to make points of contact.

Teach Truth

Currently the church is not doing well in providing sufficient Christian teaching to African Christians. The teaching should enable Christians to know the Bible and to understand fully the salvation they have in Christ, so that they can trust in Christ and obediently remain in him. Then, even in times of difficulties Christians in Africa will have the knowledge they need to seek Christ's help and will not have to go back to the ancestors and other spirits for help and guidance.

As I have argued, the book of Colossians is an excellent source of teaching on spirits because it does not deny the existence of spiritual powers, but rather it shows that Christ has power over the spirits. Colossians teaches that he created the spirits and that their power is granted by Christ himself (Col 1:15–17). In an African context, the ranks of spiritual powers include African spirits. The incarnation, death, and resurrection of Christ, as discussed in the book of Colossians, elevate Christ into a greater role than that of the spirits. Jesus Christ alone is the truth and the way to God (John 14:6). He has assumed authority in heaven and is the mediator between God and human beings, the role that the ancestors have played for many Africans. Therefore, African Christians no longer need to appeal to ancestors and spirits. On Earth, as the only source of life, Christ Jesus continuously nourishes both the physical and spiritual life of believers, and in him Christians can find everything they need for spiritual and physical blessings and security (Col 2:2–10).

Paul forbids the worship of spirit powers (Col 2:18) because only the triune God is worthy of worship and nothing else, visible or invisible, on earth or in the heavens should share this honour with God. Thus, African Christians do not need to worship spirits.

Provide a Context for Teaching Truth

As well as teaching biblical truth, the church in Africa also needs to teach Christian knowledge in a way that enables people to relate their Christian faith to their world. This can be done without falling into syncretism by emphasizing the aspects of the gospel that are most important to African Christians, by using methods that are familiar to Africans and by developing rituals that meet people's emotional needs. If the church does this, then African Christians will not continue to find Christianity foreign, and they will be helped to lead a suitable and faithful life according to their context.

As discussed, the church in Africa must provide pastoral help to African Christians so they understand that Jesus does meet their day to day needs and that he overcomes the power of the spirits who create difficult situations. This can be done in a variety of ways, including ceremonies for important occasions, power encounters, and small groups. Small groups for Bible studies can be encouraged in each congregation because they give people an opportunity to get to know one another better than they can when the whole congregation meets. Testimonies from those who use small groups for Bible studies show that there is freedom of expression and a desire to work together. In small groups, people encourage one another in prayer and advise one another. During small group Bible studies, the group can discuss issues in life and find and implement practical.

As suggested in chapter 5, incorporating good traditional values in the practice of the church is meaningful. By using tangible things that are common to local people, such as water for the Maasai, priests can bless Christians in their traditional ways in the name of Christ. It is also biblical for the church to permit elders or heads of families to confer Christian blessings on members of their families. When they are praying for local Christians, pastors and Christians can use Christian symbols, such as a cross, as a sign of the presence of Christ. Symbols help people to focus on the presence of the power of Christ himself. This will enable the gospel of Christ to be meaningful to the everyday lives of local people. We need, however, to do all these with great care so that we do not use Christian symbols magically and, thus, misrepresent the truth and supremacy of the power of Christ. We should also not incorporate traditional rituals that will lead us outside our Christian faith and, thus, disappoint our God.

Provide an African Training Context

If all these changes are to happen, we need ministers who thoroughly understand what the contextualisation and indigenisation of Christianity for Africans is all about. Currently most ministers have received Western-orientated theological training that does not deal with African traditional life. Therefore, there is great need for a contextualised curriculum for training church ministers in Africa so they become fully equipped with positive and adequate biblical and African anthropological responses to meet the needs of Christians. With this contextual theological knowledge, as the comparative study of Colossians showed, ministers will be able to discern what makes a biblical message relevant and how to relate the gospel to the spiritual world of Africans. It should be the message of salvation from sins and of assurance that Christ's power frees Christians from the influence of evil supernatural powers and helps them to solve their daily problems. With this contextual theological knowledge, ministers will not condemn Christians who revert to traditional religious practices, especially in times of crisis. Instead, the ministers will pastorally offer Christian alternatives to their issues. Ministers will have the ability to relate the gospel to real life of Christians in the context of the societies in which they live. By doing so local Christians will appreciate God's salvation in Christ.

With contextual biblical teaching, church ministers would see the importance of providing Christian teaching to their congregations in meaningful ways. This will help African Christians discern good values in their traditional religious heritage and how to make use of then practices in the church.

Do More Research

The church in African needs to take another step to deal with the impact of spiritism on the church. More research is needed into the ways in which African traditional beliefs and practice influence local Christians today. This book has shown, by using an example from the book of Colossians and from interviews with Christians and non-Christians, how issues like this can be addressed biblically and relevantly. There is a pressing need for further study in other areas of African traditional practices like the various religious and social orders and taboos, and ceremonies and rites, such as initiations, circumcisions and marriage. The importance of these needs to be researched carefully and in detail so that good values of traditional practices can be adapted into the church to enrich its teaching and practices. This is what contextualization of the gospel message into the life of local people is all about.

APPENDIX I

Biblical Truths Regarding Spirits and Ancestors

By giving people a biblical understanding of spirits, the church will start to correct the problems caused by ignoring spirits, especially in their traditional role as mediators with God and as the sources of blessing. The main points to cover regard to spirits of any kind are the following:

- Evil spirits and the spirits of the dead invisibly inhabit the world and have great influence upon those who believe in them. The spirits of the dead remember what took place during their lives and they seem to have additional knowledge, as revealed when Moses and Elijah spoke with Jesus (Luke 9:31). The story of the rich man and the beggar Lazarus also indicates that the dead are knowledgeable about the real situation on earth (Luke 16:27–31) and can convey messages as the appearance of Samuel to King Saul indicates (1 Sam 28:14–20).
- These spirits are powerless to hurt Christians, who live under the lordship of Jesus Christ.

- All types of spirits are inferior to Jesus Christ because he created them and they are subject to his supreme power.
- Jesus Christ has replaced the mediatory function of ancestors.
- Jesus Christ, by coming to earth and by his death and resurrection, has assumed a singular importance. He is lord and judge over all living and dead, including the spirits. Thus, ancestors and other spirits are cut off, as means of blessing and Christians are to lay their power line to Christ.

This however, does not mean that those who belong to Christ are to disrespect the ancestors.

- Honouring parents and the elderly in the community is biblical.
- This submission is not applicable to ancestors who are dead. We can remember their characters and advice and respect them. This should be by living holy lives of godly character and behaviour, by honouring the good works done by dead relatives h and by walking in their faiths, if they were Christians.
- We must be careful when we honour our dead elderly and relatives that we do not return to the beliefs and practices of spirits. The Bible warns us against consulting the dead for whatever reason. We should not look to any ancestor and spirit for

guidance, correction or help or for blessing upon our lives.

- We must look only to God, through Jesus Christ for all our needs. We must pray to God in the name of Jesus Christ and He will certainly help us according to the need we have.

BIBLIOGRAPHY

Arnold, Clinton E. *The Colossian Syncretism*, Grand Rapids: Baker Books, 1996.

Bediako, Kwame. 'Christian Religion and the African World-view: Will Ancestors Survive?' *Christianity in Africa: The Renewal of Non-Western Religion*, Edinburgh University Press, pp 210-233, 1995.

Bruce, F. F. *The Epistles to the Colossians, Philemon and to the Ephesians*. Grand Rapids: Wm. B. Eerdmans Publishing Co.,1998.

Bujo, Benezel. *African Theology in its Social Context* Maryknoll, New York: Orbis Books, 1992.

Burnett, David. *World of Spirits*. London: Monarch Books, 2000.

Dickson, Kwesi A. *Theology in Africa*. Maryknoll, New York: Orbis Books, 1984.

Dunn, James. *The Epistle to the Colossians and to Philemon*. Grand Rapids: Wm. B. Eerdmans Publishing Company, 1996.

Ela, Jean. *My Faith as an African*. Maryknoll, New York: Orbis Books, 1999.

Gehman, Richard J. *African Traditional Religion in Biblical*

Perspective. Nairobi: East African Educational Publishers, 2002.

Gehman, Richard J. *Who Are The Living-Dead?* Nairobi: Evangel Publishing House, 1999.

Gibellini, Rosino. *Paths of African Theology London*: SCM Press, 1994.

Healey, Joseph & Sybertz, Donald. *Towards an African Narrative Theology*. Nairobi: Pauline Publications Africa, 1997.

Hillman, Eugene. *Towards an African Christianity: Inculturation Applied*. Mahwah: Paulist Press, 1993.

Hughes, Kent R. *Colossians and Philemon: The Supremacy of Christ*. Illinois: Crossway Books, 1999.

Kirwen, Michael C. *The Missionary and Diviner. Contending Theologies of Christian and African Religions*. Maryknoll, New York: Orbis Books, 1987.

Kuster, Volker. *The Many Faces of Jesus Christ*. Maryknoll, New York: Orbis Books, 1999.

Lane, A. N. S. *The Unseen World*. Grand Rapids: Paternoster Press, 1996.

Lucas, D. *The Message of Colossians and Philemon*. Leicester: IVP, 2000.

Magesa, Laurent. *African Religion. The Moral Traditions of Abundant Life*. New York: Orbis Books, 1997.

Magesa, Laurent. *The Prophetic Role of the Church in Tanzania Today*. Eldoret: Gaba, 1991.

Martin, R. P. *Colossians: The Church's Lord and the Christian's Liberty*. Exeter: The Paternoster Press, 1972.

Mbiti, John S. *Bible and Theology in African Christianity*. Oxford: Oxford University Press, 1986.

Mbiti, John S. *Christianity and Traditional Religions in Africa*, 1970.

Mbiti, J. *Introduction to African Religion*. London: Heinemann,1978.

Molyneux, Gordon. *Differing African Responses to the Spirit World: the Main Line Churches and Independent Churches*. Unpublished, 2001.

Moreau, A. S. *The World of the Spirits: A Biblical Study in the African Context*. Nairobi: Evangel Publishing House, 1990.

Moreau, A. S., et al eds. *Deliver us from Evil*. California: MARC World Vision Publications, 2002.

Ngewa, Samuel., et al eds. *Issues in African Christian Theology*. Nairobi: East African Educational. Publishers, 1998.

Nyamiti, Charles. *African Theology: Its culture, problems and methods*. Kampala: GABA Publications, 1973.

Nyamiti, Charles. *Christ as our Ancestors: Christology from African Perspectives*. Gwero: Mambo Press, 1984.

O'Brien, Timothy P. *Colossians, Philemon. Word Biblical Commentary 44*. England: Word Publishing, 1987.

O'Donovan, Wilbur. *Biblical Christianity in African Perspective*. Carlisle.UK: The Paternoster Press, 1996.

Okure, T; van Thiel, Paul, et al. eds. 32 *Articles Evaluating Inculturation of Christianity in Africa*. Eldoret, Kenya: EMECEA Gaba Publications, 1990.

Opoku, O. *Ancestral Curses*. Accra: Pentecost Press, 1994.

Patzia, Arthur G. Ephesians, Colossians, Philemon (NIBC). Massachusetts: Hendrickson, 1990.

Peterson, D. A. *'Spirit Possession among the Maasai in Tanzania' Africa Theological Journal.* Vol. 14:3 pp 174-178, 1985.

Priest Jr., D. *Doing Theology with Maasai.* Pasadena, California: William Carcy Library, 1990.

Rhodes, Ron. *Counterfeit Christ of the New Age Movement.* London: Baker, 1990.

Schreiter, Robert J. *Faces of Jesus in Africa.* London: SCM Press, 1992.

Schweizer, E. *The Letter to the Colossians.* London :SPCK, 1982.

Taber, C. *'The limits of indigenisation in Theology' Missiology: An International Review.* Vol VI, No 1. January pp 53-79, 1978.

Vahakangas, Mika. *In Search of Foundations for African Catholicism.* Boston: Brill, 1999.

Wall, R. W. *Colossians and Philemon. Leicester*: Leicester, 1993.

Wessels, A. *Images of Christ.* London: SCM Press, 1990.

Wright, Nicholas T. *Colossians and Philemon.* (TNT). Grand Rapids: Wm B. Eerdmans Publishing Co., 1986.

AFRICA
STUDY
BIBLE
NLT